To
Jane and Chris
With all my love
Zoe †
x x

All Patients
Great and Small

Tales of a rural District Nurse

ZOË C LLOYD

BALBOA.
PRESS
A DIVISION OF HAY HOUSE

Balboa Press books may be ordered through booksellers or by contacting:

Balboa Press
A Division of Hay House
1663 Liberty Drive
Bloomington, IN 47403
www.balboapress.com
1 (877) 407-4847

Printed in the United States of America.

ISBN: 978-1-4525-8456-0 (sc)
ISBN: 978-1-4525-8458-4 (hc)
ISBN: 978-1-4525-8457-7 (e)

Library of Congress Control Number: 2013918407

Balboa Press rev. date: 10/31/2013

Table of Contents

For J's blind faith in me

Foreword

"Do you every get that feeling when you want to describe how much you absolutely and unequivocally love and admire someone and then...you just can't.

Even though you are historically articulate, and despite the fact that you are intimate with words, that words usually tumble out, beautifully, loquaciously, deliciously and all in the right order. But... on this occasion you just can't.

People say tell me about Zoe, write a few words for Zoe, what is the essence of Zoe.

You search your intuition to find the right words, but you *just* can't.

I am the right man to ask. Definitely; I am the right man because I love her.

I am the prefect choice to write this forward, be in no doubt about that, because I am over spilling with awe and admiration for Zoe. And I have written hundreds of thousands of words, in books, in articles, in films, in plays. I know about words. I know how to make words siiiiing!

I have spoken for countless hours, in front of countless people, in countless towns and cities and countries around the world.

I am known for my ability to sculpt words.

But when people ask me about Zoe words abandon me.

All I can find is this swelling emotion in my heart. And a broad smile. And one phrase: *words are not enough—you really need to meet her.*

This wonderful, personal, emotional book is your first chance to do just that.

And hopefully it will be followed by many more books, because this gorgeous lady with her diamond body has a lot to say, all of it elixir.

Writing this foreword is a great honour for me. I feel like I am introducing the world to the next big thing."

Geoff Thompson—BAFTA winning writer.

Preface

'You should write a book!'
And so I did.

Over the years, I lost count of the number of times that I heard those words, and so began the obsession. However, the question remained as to what type of book I would write. With several previous episodes of 'burnout' to my name and thousands of hours invested in attempting to work out why, the obvious choice appeared to be a 'self-help' title.

But then I could not shift a serious questioning of whether we honestly needed any more well-meaning accounts of personal torment to add to the already burgeoning section in the bookshop. In recent years, the 'self-help' section has become the place where, for those seeking solutions to very normal issues, it is much like moths being drawn towards the light, and it is indeed a rarity to find this well-thumbed section devoid of anguished souls, who gather in the vague hope that perhaps their favourite celebrity will hold the solution to their latest problem.

That is not to say that I am not myself a huge fan of the section that houses some incredible titles and some exceptional authors; our local bookshops have offered me discounted bed and breakfast rates to camp out next to their self-help books. However, what I have come to understand is that we are all going to experience our own life lessons. No amount of reading can prevent pain and suffering. Pain and suffering is as much a part of the deal that we call 'life' as is joy and happiness. Life is about balance. Emotional balance—and accepting both pain and joy—will enable us to expose ourselves to the full kaleidoscope of experiences on offer.

The words '—self-help' convey a particular message to us. Interestingly, when reversed, 'help-self' communicates—certainly to me—a more accurate description of what life asks of us, throughout our lifetime. Age, they say, is a great leveller, and only time and experience have taught me that we learn our life lessons from one another's experiences. Reading, listening, and watching some of life's greatest teachers, philosophers, poets, and artists—both alive and deceased—has enriched my own, unfolding, purpose, and I have come to appreciate that all of our experiences are not random or coincidental. Our lives entwine to form part of an incredible tapestry.

Among some of my greatest teachers have been my patients. Each one has taught me how his or her unique path through life has demonstrated—sometimes obviously and at other times subtly—what his or her existence and purpose here was all about. Each one of us has a story to tell. Within the following chapters you will be introduced to a number of people who each has a lesson to draw upon. Their stories—in keeping with life in general—contain a full range of emotions, including humour, sadness, and hope. I hope you, the reader, enjoy reading their tales as much as I have enjoyed relating them.

Zoë C Lloyd
September 2013
Cheshire, England

Acknowledgements

Thank you to the following beautiful souls: You have each played a unique part in the book that you hold in your hands. Thank you Jan Williams for your unconditional love and support; without you I doubt that I would have weathered some of the most trying times of my life. I treasure our amazing life together. To my amazing parents, Ray and Dee, you represent everything that is good about life, and I remain in awe of your love for each other and that which you have bestowed upon me. Never once did you doubt my attempts as a novice writer, and I am eternally grateful for your unrelenting support. Gratitude also to my adopted Nan, Amy, who puts up with my constant teasing. 'I love you, you old bugger.'

Thanks also to the multi-talented and inspirational Geoff Thompson, who supported my ideas and understood my passion to write, even when I had my doubts. We share something special, and I thank God for bringing us together in a unique way. As is so accurately encapsulated in the Bhuddist Proverb: 'When the student is ready, the teacher appears.' I am inspired by you and your gracious and gentle, philanthropic ways (and—Oh!—your films and books aren't half good as well!). You undoubtedly acted as the catalyst for great change in my life and in the lives of so many others, and for that I love you more than you know. For Sharon, thank you for being Geoff's beautiful wife and soulmate. I know that you are a huge part of Geoff's incredible journey.

To John, thanks for creating such amazing illustrations for the aforementioned books by 'Geoff Thompson'. I knew intuitively that it had to be you to bring the characters of this book to life. What life you brought to this book.

Heartfelt thanks must go to two of the most amazing teachers I have ever studied with—Dr Robert Holden and Dr David Hamilton. This book has been shaped in a large respect by their teaching, love, and friendship.

Dr Robert Holden, whose passion and desire to share the fundamental teachings on love to as many as possible through his spoken and written word, is a joy to behold. His teaching has, without doubt, contributed enormously to the way that I live my life, allowing love to be my guide. Robert Holden is a treasure beyond compare; this decision is definitely not affected by his devotion to Macclesfield Town Football Club, after, of course, his beloved West Ham United, in any way!

During the last couple of years I have also been blessed to find yet another amazing teacher. Dr David Hamilton made the challenging switch from organic chemistry, working within the pharmaceutical industry, to becoming a pioneer in the mind-body field. He self-published his first book, and he went on to become one of Hay House's leading authors of multiple books. His gentle, humorous teaching of the complicated-made-simple and his excitement and thirst for more knowledge is truly infectious. He, too, is fascinated by the subject of self-love, and at present he is focusing his attention on its significance through his workshops, lectures, and writing. He is an inspiration to me and to so many others.

I wrote a considerable chunk of this book while being supplied with hot tea and coffee at two of my favourite cafes. To Louise and all of the staff at Miola in Sandbach, and to all of those at the very aptly named Food For Thought Bakery in Haslington, please accept my genuine thanks for putting up with my near permanent presence. A special mention must go to Jo, who even mopped around me at closing time!

To Shaz, Sue, Tony and Pat, Cate and Pete, Lee and Judy, and Jeanette, thank you for believing in me, and for the continued support.

Friends and family are too numerous to mention, but you know who you are, and so do I. know that I love and treasure you all.

To the staff and patients that bring this book to life.

To all involved at Balboa Press for taking my ideas, co-creating this book and bringing it to life.

Introduction

'Nothing's Real but Love' is the profound title to a truly soulful, exquisitely executed, piece of music by English singer-songwriter Rebecca Ferguson.

You may ask why it is that such few words can convey such power. The answer is that we instinctively know that when all of our attitudes and beliefs are stripped away, it is what we were born with. In other words, it is our birthright. When we look at a newborn, what is it that enchants us so much? What we witness is pure and made up of love, not yet affected by the world she has been born into. She is unaffected as yet by what she will hear, see, and otherwise be exposed to. She is totally unaware of concepts and meanings that we take for granted and that shape our lives.

As the following characters of *All Patients Great and Small* reveal themselves to you, spare a thought—regardless of their personalities—for love. It will be easy to extend our loving feelings towards some characters, while with others, it will be harder.

Ask yourself why that is? What is it that makes some of the characters who are a reflection of humankind in general so loveable, and why don't we hold those same feelings for them all?

We will follow up on this question after you have shared in their stories, and then I will give you my take on an answer.

All I ask is that you open your heart to each and every one of them and keep in mind these wise words:

<u>Children Learn What They Live</u>

Dorothy Law Nolte

If children live with criticism,
They learn to condemn.
If children live with hostility,
They learn to fight.
If children live with ridicule,
They learn to be shy.
If children live with shame,
They learn to feel guilty.
If children live with encouragement,
They learn confidence.
If children live with tolerance,
They learn to be patient.
If children live with praise,
They learn to appreciate.
If children live with acceptance,
They learn to love.
If children live with approval,
They learn to like themselves.
If children live with honesty,
They learn truthfulness.
If children live with security,
They learn to have faith in themselves and others.
If children live with friendliness,
They learn the world is a nice place in which to live.

CHAPTER 1

The story of a broken heart

Harry was an incredible man. My first encounter with Harry was as a newly appointed District Nurse to a small, rural practice on the Cheshire/Shropshire border. My colleagues had explained to me that this ninety-plus-year-old gentleman was quite unusual, and I was to discover that Harry was indeed one of a kind.

A modern cul-de-sac dotted with a selection of elegant homes hid Harry's dilapidated old property from the main road. My first visit to his home resulted in me driving straight past it, as an overgrown copse of trees shielded his drive. Without knowing that there was a property behind these trees, it was virtually impossible to find, and Harry loved it that way, as time and circumstances had resulted in him becoming semi-reclusive. Unusual for a man of his age, he was more than six feet in height and remained extremely agile. He also held a driver's licence and continued to drive to visit his older sister, who lived in an adjoining village.

He thirsted for knowledge, and he regularly shared with me the latest newsworthy items from the international science magazine *New Scientist,* which he had an annual subscription to. I vividly remember him discussing with me the new human immunodeficiency virus (HIV) therapy that was in its infancy at the time and asking me my opinion, knowing that I had previously worked as an HIV specialist nurse.

As you can imagine, it is a huge part of the patient-nurse relationship to chat, but 'Harry's topics' were often unusual, to say the least. During my visits we would often discuss the latest scientific facts. Harry had the stereotypical appearance of a wise, old, eccentric professor, and he would not have looked out of place as an old don at Oxford.

His home matched his character. Walking into the entrance hall was quite a shock to the system, with a lifetime of belongings piled to the rafters and every bit of available space accounted for. I had been informed by my predecessor that Harry was quite an inventor and, indeed, he had several patents to his name. It was well known among the staff that what is termed as 'clinical waste' could not be left for Harry to dispose of. Harry, like many people of his generation, had survived two world wars and did not like to waste anything that he felt could be recycled.

Having an open fire is very useful for disposing of waste material following dressing a wound, and Harry would state that later, after I and the other accompanying medical staff had gone, he would light his fire and ensure the incineration of his waste. We were, however, informed by his home help that, frequently, as soon as we left, Harry would open the sealed bag and rescue anything he felt that he could recycle. One such item was the plastic inner spindle that was designed to house a medicated paste bandage. After collecting several of these over a few weeks, they were used to strengthen the end of a hosepipe adapted to water his hanging baskets.

Our main reason for visiting Harry was his chronic leg ulcers. Leg ulcers are a common occurrence in old age, and for many they can be a source of huge distress, commonly causing social isolation, pain, and, frequently, embarrassment. Significant improvements in treatment and management have gone a long way to reducing this situation.

With Harry's usual zest for life, he wanted to play his part in healing the leg ulcers. Exercise of the calf muscle to improve circulation was never far from Harry's thoughts, and it came as no surprise when one day he unveiled his latest invention—a home-made exercise bike. It would be impossible to describe the bike, as to this day I have never seen anything to compare it with. A lifetime's collection of assorted nuts, bolts, coat hangers, bits of scrap metal, and a cushion for the seat had somehow been welded and soldered together to form a fully functional exercise bike. To see Harry in action on the bike was a sight to behold. God knows what a health and safety inspector would have made of it. It would challenge any site of scientific significance. Only seeing the Taj Mahal comes close to it for me! Determination and creativity drove this wonderful man.

Harry had remained a confirmed bachelor following the suicide of his sweetheart. He had met this lady, Jane, while recovering in the hospital following a near fatal motorbike accident. With tears in his eyes, Harry shared with me their tragic story. Jane was a newly qualified Irish staff nurse, and one of her regular duties involved dressing the sizeable leg wound that Harry had sustained during the crash. The consultant in charge of Harry's care was eager to amputate the lower leg because of an infection. As a young man at the time it is hard to contemplate the fear that this must have created in Harry. Jane, however, was quite determined to continue with the dressing regime and encouraged Harry to actively refuse the consultant's suggestion. The wound resulted in a several-month stay in the hospital on bed rest, and during this time the two became close. Upon his discharge, Harry asked Jane out, and she agreed to a date.

Their romance blossomed and ultimately led to engagement. Unfortunately, Sectarian conflict was very active in Ireland at the time, and Jane's father was a staunch Catholic. Harry's Protestant beliefs were not recognised by her father, and Jane's father's drastic response was to forbid the couple's relationship. Jane was sent away to America to fulfil a nursing position. Despite every effort by Harry to reassure Jane that he would in time join her in America, depression ensued for Jane, and within a few months she had committed suicide.

I have often heard the expression used that someone 'died of a broken heart', but this is one of the times that no other description comes closer. When Harry talked about Jane, it was with immense affection, a deep sadness, and the haunted look of a man who had truly lost a soulmate. Despite a period of approximately seventy years, the leg that I now had responsibility for dressing had survived, and I felt a humble connection with Jane. I admired and respected her for what she had managed to achieve.

Harry's other love was nature and, particularly, wildlife. He had an amazing rapport with birds, and I remember on several occasions walking into his lounge and feeling that I had somewhat intruded on his conversations with his resident male blackbird. The bird was often found sitting on the back of Harry's armchair, taking food by hand. He rarely stayed more than a few conciliatory seconds when anyone else entered the room, exiting through the window that was left open for him.

Unfortunately, this special relationship was to cause some unforeseen problems over time. The blackbird, like the majority of his kind, eventually found a mate, and this relationship naturally led to a brood of chicks. Harry enjoyed witnessing the enchanting antics of the first brood as they fledged. Unfortunately, an unwelcome visitor to the nest was a magpie and, as is customary with these birds, it was to attack the next brood, killing some of the chicks. Harry witnessed this act with some distress, and after seeing how helpless the parents were in deterring the perpetrator of these deeds, he decided to take the law into his own hands. Having been a crack shot amateur marksman as a younger man, Harry remained the licensed holder of a shotgun. The unsuspecting magpie was to get little warning of his intended fate and, as the bird flew into Harry's garden, a direct hit saw the instant demise of the bird. The problem for Harry was that the bird landed in the garden of his next-door neighbour, and, within the space of an hour, the local village bobby was knocking on Harry's door, demanding an explanation. Being an honest gentleman in every sense of the word, Harry described the plight of the blackbirds. Knowing the local policeman myself, I guessed that a part of him was extremely touched by Harry's endeavours to protect this tiny family. Unfortunately, however, as a law enforcer, he was unable to show approval of Harry's 'vigilante' actions. Harry had held a gun licence for the whole of his adult life, and despite this new evidence that he remained a crack shot; the policeman was concerned that the incident highlighted the need for a re-application of his licence.

It was so sad to witness the huge impact that this had on Harry's quality of life. It made me think of the significance that we individually place on things that to another may have little or no appeal. Unfortunately, for Harry this marked the general decline in his well-being. Having only risen to the dizzy heights of owning a spud gun and a water pistol as a child, I was not acquainted with the process that was to be followed when applying for a new gun licence. The medical practice became involved, with my GP colleague having to make the decision as to whether Harry was suitable to hold a gun licence. Harry's vision and other senses were scrutinised, and, unfortunately, the GP had to make the difficult decision that he could not recommend that the licence be renewed. It brought a lump to my throat and that of my medical colleague to explain the reasoning to Harry. With tears in his eyes it was heart breaking to see this stoical gentleman plead with the GP to grant him his licence. I vividly remember him telling the GP that as long as he could remember he had owned a gun and that he promised he would never use the gun again if he could be granted permission to own a firearm.

It was with a very heavy heart that I allowed Harry his privacy to come to terms with the news. During the next few months I witnessed a sad decline in Harry's health that he and I both recognised was because of his loss of his right to keep his guns. He described it as 'knocking the first nail in his coffin'. Our future relationship remained positive, but the intimate nurse–patient bond that we had shared had been severely affected, and Harry never wholly trusted me in the future.

This remains a dilemma for many community nurses who share a somewhat unique opportunity to become a huge part in someone's life. The boundaries can become extremely blurred at times, and I have spent many hours ruminating over the well-being of a patient, much like a mother over her children. At the end of Harry's life he was to become bedridden for a short while. We respected his wishes, which were to allow a minimum number of staff to attend him at this vulnerable time. I was honoured to be one of these few. Before a brief period of unconsciousness and during one of our last meetings, Harry shared with me an incredible memory, and it is with this story that I choose to finish the chapter.

Harry remembered a time as a small boy when the circus came to town. This, as you can imagine, was a great treat for the children of a small village that was ten miles from a town.

The young Harry found out that an elephant that was part of the show had sadly died unexpectedly. This must have posed a real dilemma with regard to disposing of the carcass, and, thus, the deceased animal had to be left for a few days until appropriate arrangements could be made to bring lifting gear to the site of the circus. While the remains were still in the village, Harry and a friend of his decided that they would make further investigations. A pair of ladders was strategically placed against the elephant's side, and the boys were able to climb up the elephant and stand on top of the creature. The boy's curiosity led them to examine the deceased animal bit by bit.

Harry vividly described the trampoline-like properties that the elephant's large side provided. During the next few hours the boys happily entertained themselves bouncing on their accommodating host.

It is hard to imagine the chaos that later ensued when the decomposing carcass gave way under the weight of the young pals, and they found themselves being rescued by the local fire service. Young Harry had become caught in the ribcage of the deceased elephant, and it was left to his young accomplice to summon help. Harry's vivid description of the rescue mission was not a story for those with a delicate constitution!

As a natural wildlife enthusiast with enormous respect for all animals, Harry had mixed feelings regarding his close encounter with this beautiful animal. In an attempt to ease Harry's conscience, I reminded him that, at the tender age of ten, like all young boys of that number of years, mischief is part of the territory, and he had in his adult life more than made up for his early misdemeanours with the animal world.

CHAPTER 2

Animal husbandry

Any community nurse is well acquainted with the fact that at times she will be required to multi-task. What it does not state in the job description is that there will be a need to have attended advanced animal behaviour training. Anyone with an aversion to dogs or cats should definitely not apply for a District Nurse post. During the interview process, among the questions addressed to the candidates should be those along the lines of whether they are prepared to deal with cleaning up after a host of animals, and whether they have a flea repellent spray in their medicine cabinet.

As an animal lover, the important role that patients' pets play in their lives comes as no surprise to me. It would be difficult to relate the number of occasions where I have witnessed an incredible bond between a patient and his or her pet. It is not unusual to meet elderly people who refuse to go into residential or nursing homes because it would mean leaving their beloved pets.

Animals in a rural village come in all shapes and sizes. I have had the rare privilege of various animals being named in my honour, among them being a calf, a cocker spaniel, and a chipmunk. Hearing, 'Zoë, come here now, you naughty girl!' has had me turning around on more than one occasion. The announcement that their pet reminds them of you is at first a shock to the system; realising that you share the attributes of a chipmunk could be the end of a burgeoning ego.

However, on reflection, I remember how Enid, a charming patient who had advanced bowel cancer, quite enjoyed regaling her stories about my name sake. 'She's so like you, Sister,' she would share with me on my visits. 'Never still she is—always on the go. Goes mad when anyone visits like she's really pleased to see them. And makes such a fuss of me.' How couldn't I be touched by such a backhanded compliment?

I remember meeting the newborn calf that was less than a day old when it was named in my honour. Thoughts of what health and safety rules would have to say about being in a stable were pushed to the back of my mind as I went in plastic apron in situ to become acquainted with this beautiful newborn. What I was not prepared for was the strength of suckling that was bestowed upon my fingers. A rough tongue and a slimy mouth were two features I hoped we did not share! This young female calf was born into a large herd of Friesian cows and would remain at the farm, unlike the males that were taken away to market.

I do not remember being told during my interview that experience in sheep herding would be advantageous, but I remember vividly my initiation into this art on an extremely wet and windy Wednesday afternoon. With the exception of myself because I was fulfilling the role of the District Nurse, all staff shared the luxury of a half-day on a Wednesday. As the staff departed with smiles and tales of what lovely treats they had in store for their afternoon, I began to sense what a sad-eyed spaniel feels like when left with a conciliatory chew stick and a concessionary pat on the head as everyone else heads off without even a backward glance. My only reward was that I was considered to be responsible enough and of sufficient seniority to have a key to the surgery, allowing me access to the office and providing some much needed, undisturbed, time to catch up on paperwork (the bane of my life).

And so it was that I was for once relishing the thought of spending the afternoon in a warm and cosy office, as outside the stormy weather showed no signs of letting up, when the sound of the surgery doorbell and some frantic shouting alerted me to what was an obvious emergency. Standing at the surgery door was an extremely distressed young farmer, who quickly explained that his father had collapsed and had stopped breathing.

I was led to an enormous farm vehicle on the adjacent car park—not the most practical of vehicles to gain access to in a nurse's dress. With an assisted push on my rear, I was soon in the cab performing cardiopulmonary resuscitation (CPR), to be quickly joined by the community physiotherapist, whose mobile unit was parked on the car park. Despite our best efforts, we were unable to save the life of this gentleman, and the arriving paramedic staff confirmed this fact. The young farmer was aware that I had been nursing his grandmother for some time and asked if I would come back to the family's farm and break the news to his mother and the rest of his family. Less accustomed to sudden death in my role, and without my GP colleagues, I was naturally out of my comfort zone but felt responsible under the circumstances to honour this request.

Breaking the news of a sudden death often results in initial disbelief because of shock. What many may consider to be an inappropriate response because of this shock is extremely common. As I sat down with the wife of the deceased, upon hearing the devastating news, her first response was, 'Who will get the sheep in?' At first I didn't realise that this was a genuine concern, but after the initial pot of tea, which in our culture is customary following bad news, again the welfare of the sheep was mentioned. Any nurse will confirm that when we have to deliver catastrophic news following the 'kettle being put on' our next natural response is to offer help.

'What can I do to help?' was, on this occasion, genuinely met with, 'Can you get the sheep in?'

As the son of the deceased had been dispatched to inform other close family members of the death, it fell to me to step up to the challenge. The raging storm seemed to be mocking this novice sheep herder, as, in failing light, equipped with a torch, a borrowed oversized waterproof, and a pair of wellington boots that would have fit Bigfoot, I less than enthusiastically headed off down the fields into unknown territory.

In prayer at this point, I called upon the spirit of my deceased farming grandparents to offer any welcome guidance from beyond the grave.

I now have total respect when I watch *One Man and His Dog* on television, as I quickly discovered that, without the control of a faithful hound, it is almost a total impossibility to get sheep to all head in the same direction. Considering the old saying that 'we all follow like sheep', I have decided it should have an addition that states 'but not necessarily in the same direction'.

After what seemed like an age, the entire flock of sheep and I had managed to find our way back to the barn, and—cold, wet, and bedraggled—I was prepared to return to the farm house. I felt exhausted. Going to the gym or even playing Wii Fit has nothing on sheep herding, which must burn off calories like no other exercise. I was, however, feeling very proud of my new skill, and the phrase 'we aim to please' sprung to mind as I sat down with the gathering family who thanked me for my assistance.

What this event taught me was that often what we as nurses perceive to be the most appropriate actions are not necessarily those of our patients and their family members. I am not for a minute suggesting that as part of our training we include herding farm animals, but it does demonstrate the unique and privileged role that we play in the lives of the members of our communities.

CHAPTER 3

A tall story

There is nothing quite like an eccentric character to make the long shifts more bearable. Dick was a perfect example, and he epitomised what makes a tightly knit small community a unique place to work. Before retirement, Dick had been the village gravedigger, a role that he was extremely proud of. Before a decline in his health affected his mobility, he was often to be found in the local graveyard surveying the newly dug graves with the scrutiny of one who knows the intricacies of such a craft.

Prone to 'embellish the truth', shall we say, Dick's stories were regarded as classic tales, and my medical and nursing colleagues alike always looked forward to his latest ramblings.

My first encounter with Dick was to assess an itchy foot rash. My GP colleague had passed the responsibility to me, as often happens in district nursing, smelly feet not being high on a GP's agenda it would appear. On this occasion, it was a wise move on his part, as the inside of Dick's boot was not a pretty sight. The odour was enough to knock even the strongest 'cast-iron' stomach off course. As I unlaced Dick's boots and slowly and carefully removed his sodden socks, it occurred to me that Dick's feet had not seen daylight in a good while. Faced with what I can only describe as terribly neglected feet, which were both pungent smelling and wet, Dick excitedly proceeded to give me his considered diagnosis. Patients often offer their own suggestions regarding the possible nature and cause of the diseases with which they are inflicted, and, as 'the patient knows best', they are usually somewhat accurate.

Dick had the most expressive eyes, which danced with delight when he was in full flow. His extremely bushy eyebrows appeared to have a mind of their own, and they played a huge part in communicating his excitement. 'Trench foot!' he exclaimed, with a confident certainty. 'That be it, Sister. Saw plenty of it in the war!' The more excited Dick got, the more that he would repeat things, rapidly, and he would often add an 'aye' or an 'ahh' at the beginning or end of a statement. 'Aye that's what it is!' and 'Ahh that's it!'

Being relatively confident that I was confronted with a fungal foot infection, I felt that Dick's diagnosis sounded a more dramatic and newsworthy one. On reflection, while explaining to Dick my findings, I did indeed agree that despite initially having reached the conclusion of a different diagnosis, that indeed 'trench foot' and fungal foot infection were one and the same. It gave Dick huge kudos with his elderly male pals to be able to tell them that 'Sister' had agreed with his diagnosis.

I was to become a regular visitor at Dick's on and off during the next few years, and I never once tired of his 'tall stories'. Knowing that Dick was, some would say, gullible, his son-in-law regularly fed him snippets of prefabricated stories, which Dick would then eagerly share with me and my team during our regular visits. On one occasion, I vividly remember him informing me that our senior GP colleague had been included in the New Year's honours list for his work within our local community. This appeared somewhat unlikely I felt, as I had minutes before left this colleague finishing a morning surgery session. I felt sure that during our coffee break, while he signed the prescriptions, and we shared out the patient visits, such news would have been shared. Dick became totally convinced by the validity of his son-in-law's stories, however, and no amount of discussion would change his opinion. It certainly brought a smile to the GP's face in future when we referred to him and his wife by the titles of Sir Barrie and Lady Shelagh.

Like so many patients of Dick's generation, a decline in mobility often means that the visit of the nurse is an important part of their lives. Loneliness and isolation in the elderly is an increasing issue with an ageing population and the erosion of traditional established family units. Many elderly people, particularly in isolated locations, live their latter years largely alone.

Dick like a great many of his contemporaries looked forward to his visits from both the nurses and the GPs. One of the most challenging aspects to providing care at home is not to force your own standards upon that of your patients. In Dick's case, this was quite a test. The commode chair, which often doubled as an oversized spittoon, was often in pride of place in the lounge, and it was often from where Dick directed his conversations. Dick enjoyed nothing more than to greet me as I entered his home with his latest in-depth personal bowel update. The front door opened directly into the lounge, and I became accustomed to being greeted directly from his 'throne' so to speak. As any nurse will confirm, the current state of their patient's bowel pattern is often their dominant line in conversation. Accompanying grunts, groans, and contorted facial expressions only added to the picture that Dick graphically painted. I often wondered if he had a permanent seat mark across his buttocks, considering the amount of time that he spent ensconced on his 'throne'.

Despite an extremely supportive daughter, it was not easy to provide Dick with the amount of care that he required as his declining health caught up with him. Remaining in the house that he had been born in was hugely important for this engaging gentleman, who we all secretly had a soft spot for. We offered as much help and support as we could in accordance with his wishes. Like many people of his generation, he was determined that his family should inherit the family home, and despite feeling that he would be far better cared for in a residential/nursing setting, we ultimately had to respect his decision to end his days at home. When a patient is of sound mind, as Dick was, we may feel uncomfortable leaving a patient in this situation, but ultimately it is a decision that we must accept.

One of the last conversations that we engaged in involved yet another 'tall story'. It involved one of his long-time contemporaries who had lived his life in the village. With those twinkling eyes and dancing eyebrows, Dick went on to inform me that the previously mentioned GP—'He of the peerage'—had paid for his friend to immigrate to Australia, where he was to see out the remainder of his days. According to Dick, his pal had suffered with a 'bad chest' since childhood, and to assist his breathing he was off to a warmer climate to end his days. Once again, his comedic son-in-law had created yet another elaborate tale that had Dick totally hooked. While having worked with some amazingly dedicated GPs, I have yet to come across one who has been bestowed with the Royal seal of approval and who pays for and arranges emigration! Over the years I have very occasionally managed to encourage/bribe one or two GPs to brew-up, and I can honestly report that that alone was an uphill challenge of gigantic proportions.

However, for Dick, as I am sure you will appreciate, there was not a doctor on the planet who could compare to his own GP's unique abilities. Consequent of our ever-changing society and social structures, patients like Dick are, pardon the pun, 'a dying breed'. I often remember Dick and his many stories with a smile on my face.

Following his death, in line with his wishes, Dick was laid to rest in his chosen plot in his beloved graveyard. It seemed only fitting that his final resting place be where he had spent so many happy hours performing a job that was, for him, a labour of love.

CHAPTER 4

The pointlessness of prejudice

Margaret was, by traditional methods of social class classification, 'middle class'. She was also married with one adult son, who himself was a general practitioner. I was to meet her as a result of a request by the senior partner. Common to many people in their later years, she was suffering from a venous leg ulcer.

For a District Nurse this shall we say is the 'bread and butter' of our trade, and we spend a considerable proportion of our working life well acquainted with the long-term consequences of varicose veins. Pregnancy and standing occupations contribute to this all too common dilemma of old age. The cost of treating leg ulcers in monetary terms to the National Health Service and, more importantly, the personal cost to the patient, is excessive, and, for this reason, preventing the ulcer from developing or indeed from reoccurring is important. In Margaret's case, previous to the development of the ulcer, she was like many patients unaware of the potential that what starts off as an itchy, discoloured rash, referred to as varicose eczema, can potentially develop into an ulcer.

I remember vividly my first meeting with Margaret. A large, sweeping drive led me to the front of a rather grand home with accompanying, equally splendid, well-planned grounds. An immaculate, vintage Jaguar was parked in front of an adjacent detached garage. The gravel was the expensive type—deep and crunching—that you typically see outside stately homes, and on pressing the front doorbell a rather splendid chime rang out that announced my arrival.

First impressions created an image of the TV series *To the Manor Born*, and I would not have been at all surprised if a butler had appeared. The door, however, was opened by an extremely elegantly dressed, tall but slightly stooped, elderly man who introduced himself as Dennis, my patient's husband, and who told me that his wife was waiting for me in the drawing room. I was led down the grand hallway.

It is not uncommon as a District Nurse on arrival at a patient's home to have to let ourselves in, having been hollered at to enter from another part of the house. I guessed for Dennis that collecting the nurse in the manner in which I had been greeted was a well-rehearsed procedure, and time confirmed this to be true. Feeling quite overwhelmed and nervous, I hoped that these emotions did not come across as I was officially introduced to my patient.

Forming our first impressions, it is well documented, happens very quickly, and these impressions have a large impact on the future relationship, for both patient and nurse. More than half of this impression is formed purely by non-verbal communication. Intuitively, I sensed that in this particular introduction it was essential that first impressions went well. Extreme charm and politeness were extended to me, and I was invited by my host to sit down. Warnings and feelings from childhood returned rapidly; 'Don't touch 'and 'little girls should be seen and not heard,' sprung to mind.

Sitting in front of Margaret felt akin to taking tea with the aristocracy. Her demeanour spoke volumes, and I quickly learnt that presentation was extremely important. Her attention to detail was obvious, both in her personal dress sense and in her home furnishings. Within a short time of my arrival, I was served with tea, and I endeavoured to hold the best china precisely according to 'tea drinker's etiquette'. During this impromptu cup of tea, I was to learn much about Margaret's background, and I felt she wanted me to become acquainted with that that was important to her. The Conservative Party, bridge, debating current affairs, and *The Daily Telegraph* crossword were among her passions. Her opinions were important to her, and during my next few visits I was to learn that she had a very low opinion of the gay and black communities.

Put another way I didn't expect to see her lead the Gay Pride march, or appear at Notting Hill Carnival! Encountering prejudice within the nurse-patient relationship can be difficult and often challenging. I do not remember, certainly through my nurse training, discussing prejudice, and yet it is an ongoing and far-reaching topic that requires attention. I have a vivid memory of a nurse tutor during the psychiatric element of my training stating that 'homosexuals' were categorised as suffering from a psychosexual disorder, and they should be treated as such. Considering that this was during the mid-1980s, I found this a less than accurate and caring approach to a patient within our care. I don't even remember the needs of any ethnic cultures beyond the dominant one being discussed.

I am pleased to report that this is no longer the case with the discussion and exploration of prejudice forming part of the current training curriculum. Fortunately, the Nursing and Midwifery Council (the NMC), our governing body, has a clear code of conduct that assists us in tricky areas, such as how to manage potentially difficult situations.

Despite Margaret's generally gracious and cooperative behaviour during my visits, I found it difficult when she became verbally offensive regarding black or gay issues. While acknowledging that

Margaret's age, upbringing, and past experiences were bound to play a part in forming her opinions, I suspected that a great deal of her verbal tirade was largely because of her fear of the unknown, as there was virtually no obvious presence of either any black or outwardly gay people in the village that she had lived her life in.

Attitudes have changed generally, and during the last thirty years we have witnessed a shift away from this type of outspokenness. With the birth of reality TV and the inclusion of positive gay and black role models in soap operas, it is rare to encounter these strong opinions. In Margaret's particular case, during her care I would try to steer the conversation towards other topics and encourage her to share the crossword clues while I attended to her dressings.

What was sad about this otherwise pleasant lady was that she could not share in the hilariousness of her situation. On one occasion, as she regaled the distress of a 'possible gay encounter', I did not know how to suppress my laughter. Margaret had made her annual pilgrimage to the Conservative Party Conference with a female friend and co-supporter. On arrival at the hotel, the pair went to book in, only to find out that the twin-bedded room that had been booked was not available, and a double bed was all that was left at the hotel. Margaret was horrified, and this was mirrored in her recital of the event. 'I made it perfectly clear to my companion that I had never shared a bed with another woman and that I would only comply with the arrangement if a line of pillows was placed to clearly mark respective boundaries. Can you imagine if people had found out about the arrangements?' she said to me, still totally horrified by the thought.

It may sound dramatic, but you could be forgiven, even after several years, for thinking that Margaret's bedtime encounter had resulted in a diagnosis of post-traumatic stress disorder (PTSD).

During the years that I would be a visitor to this dear lady's home I was to discover the real cause of her deep-rooted opinions. Like many people with low self-esteem, she was tremendously affected by what other people thought of her. She was a victim of what I refer to as 'keeping up with the Joneses' syndrome'. Image was so important to her that she appeared to live a half-life.

Appearing to be on guard at all times, it was a state that not only must have been exhausting but that deflected away from the true substance of this wonderful soul. Fortunately, I was able to see past what she routinely presented to the world and regularly caught sight of the true essence of Margaret during my time getting to know her.

Over the years, Margaret began to succumb to health issues other than a venous leg ulcer, and, eventually, following a heart attack, she became weak and was confined to her bed. During the last few days of her life I was one of very few people who she allowed to witness her decline. She remained resplendent with exquisitely expensive nightwear and bedding. Her appearance was extremely important to her, and we reached an understanding that if and when she could not apply her own make-up and hairspray that I would perform these important rituals on her behalf. The irony was not wasted on me that I was chosen for these extremely important personal tasks.

The expression of my personality through image was just as important to me, but for very different reasons. An outward appearance of smartness and elegance was an essential way for Margaret to show herself to the world as being such; my image was to do with seeing myself as casual, relaxed, young, and fun. A quirky, spiky haircut was my signature piece, and it was a definite expression of who I was and remains so. Margaret and I were polar opposites in our outward appearances, yet the bond we shared had transcended this.

Being involved in the final days of a person's life is an extreme privilege, and the intimacy shared between nurse and the dying person's family is unlike any other experience. The two occasions on which we are most vulnerable in life are naturally around birth and death. The process of dying can be made less traumatic if the patient feels secure and safe. The presence of an experienced nurse who is known and trusted by the patient makes a massive difference, and during the last days and hours of Margaret's life as she slipped in and out of consciousness I was able to hold her hand and reassure her that I was complying with all of her expressed wishes. As Margaret took her final breath I was the only person present. As I said a final goodbye with a gentle kiss to her forehead, unusually I shed a few tears.

The tears were a representation of my sadness that in our long-term patient-nurse relationship I had never been able to share my real self with her. Being gay, while only a part of my life, was something that I never felt able to share with this wonderful lady. Previous discussions about my 'other half' were carefully orchestrated so as not to expose my partner as a female. I have often wondered how Margaret would have reacted to the news that I was not who she believed I was. Denying a part of our identity is never easy, but it can be argued that in this case the patient's needs were better met without sharing my personal circumstances.

There remains a part of me that will be forever curious as to what would have been Margaret's reaction. I would like to believe that her belief in me in every other way would have challenged her attitudes. I doubt she would have gone on to be a gay rights activist, but who knows?

CHAPTER 5

Getting fruity in the rhubarb patch

For those of us blessed with an ample bosom and who are required to wear a nurse's uniform, something it would appear takes over, or possibly 'possesses', gentlemen of a certain age when they are in our presence. Forewarned they say is forearmed, and the following case is a classic example of such.

Kenny was one of a trio of brothers who had lived and worked locally all of their lives. Over a period of years I had become acquainted with his two brothers, but for a long while I was not to meet this infamous elder brother. As is often the case in a village, rumours and gossip abounded—it is very much a part of human nature, and I was aware that this brother had a reputation for being rather a charmer with the ladies.

When the request arrived for me to visit it was done rather, shall we say, sheepishly, as the male GP knew only too well that I would be dodging the human version of an octopus. The purpose of my visit to Kenny's home was to assess and help treat very swollen legs. The GP had decided that compression socks were to be our first line of treatment, in the hope that this may prevent commencing medications. Swollen legs and the elderly are like any other double act you care to mention; it is not exactly peaches and cream, but rarely do we witness one without the other.

On my arrival it was not difficult to work out how this old-time Lothario had earned his reputation. Persuading Kenny that measuring his calves did not require removal of his underpants and trousers was akin to pushing water uphill. He claimed that he couldn't tell what I was saying, which seemed strange as he had no problem deciphering the initial message. Trying to pull up both underpants and trousers while on my knees was not an easy manoeuvre, as gravity and reluctance from Kenny to assist was hindering any progress. With a monumental effort I was eventually the winner of this dual, and with the assistance of his belt the trousers were back in their rightful position. Following this stupendous exertion, Kenny was out of breath and so was I. The measuring of his calves by comparison was a lot less strenuous. The remainder of the visit went by relatively smoothly, if not without a few invitations to become better acquainted out of work time.

Creating boundaries with over-amorous elderly gentlemen is a tricky dilemma, and it has to be managed with as much tact and compassion as possible. While it may be flattering to receive positive compliments from patients, comments such as those that make reference to our voluptuous nature can be difficult to deflect. As this visit came to a natural close, I quietly congratulated myself on keeping Kenny's suggestions at arm's length.

I did not anticipate that Kenny would save his best efforts for the point of my departure. 'Would you like some rhubarb, nurse?' seemed an innocuous enough request, and I thought was a necessary distraction as I ran the gauntlet that was the passage through from the lounge to the garden. I didn't account for Kenny's dogged determination. As I followed my patient to his rhubarb patch I was invited to choose my own produce. Clutching my freshly cut stalks with both hands I was placed at a distinct disadvantage, and Kenny's carefully planned military operation reached its pinnacle. For a relatively frail elderly gent even I was impressed with his well-executed plan, as he grabbed my breast and asked, 'How about a kiss?" I managed easily to fend off his advances, and a few sharp words were all it took to bring him back to reality, and his, 'You can't blame me for trying,' were the last words on the matter.

On my hasty departure a few minutes later we were both left to reflect on this 'fruity' encounter. Experience has taught me that events like these can be misconstrued, and some may choose to consider whether to visit such patients without a colleague accompanying them. While I would not want to put myself or another at risk of sexual harassment each case requires careful consideration.

Many patients of advanced years have outlived their spouse, and while never condoning inappropriate sexual advances, most fumbled attempts at a quick feel are immediately backed up with huge embarrassment and a humble apology. The abrupt lack of love and intimacy in a patient's life is typically the trigger to this sort of conduct. On this occasion, I had been forewarned that Kenny had a reputation for his over-amorous nature with ladies but that he presented no real risk to our safety. The following day I recounted my story to our senior GP Barrie. Barrie was always amused by the regaling of my close encounters, and this experience seemed to have him laughing even more than usual. In fact, he was laughing so hard I realised that there had to be another element to this saga.

I had just shared with him that the upside to the previous day's events was a fantastic rhubarb crumble that myself and my partner had enjoyed following our evening meal. 'You didn't eat it?' he quizzed, laughing with tears rolling down his face.

'Of course,' I replied. 'Why not?'

'Because he pees on it.'

I thought at this point that Barrie had to be joking, but I was to find out that Kenny, as well as many others, preferred to urinate on their rhubarb as an alternative to traditional customary toileting. Not being an Alan Titchmarsh-type, I was not aware at the time that there are huge benefits to the enrichment of our crops with the addition of a healthy sprinkling of human urine. It took me months to live down this tale, and indeed it still remains part of folk law within the practice.

Only recently, at Barrie's retirement party, was the event once again shared among the guests, to, as usual, draw hearty laughter from us all. Kenny's rather inappropriate toilet habits and grabbing hands had been immortalised in the surgery's history for ever more.

CHAPTER 6

The undertaker—a family affair

As the role of the nurse has undergone many changes during the last century so has that of the undertaker. As attitudes towards death have generally become less a matter of feeling fear and dread, the preparation for funerals has become for many an important part of planning to follow their wishes following the end of life. What once used to be thought of with accompanying immense trepidation is now planned with immaculate detail.

Historically, the image of the funeral director was depicted as a cold-hearted, emotionless, and creepy character. For those of us old enough to remember the BBC's comedy *Dad's Army*, the character of Frasier in this television show did nothing to enhance this reputation. My experience of the modern-day funeral director could not be further from this depiction. It is ironic that none of us are going to escape becoming acquainted with this warm-hearted group of people, as death is something common to us all.

During my early years as a District Nurse, without doubt one of the commonest questions I was asked immediately after the death of a family member would be, 'What will happen to Mum/Dad now?' Considering that we are relinquishing our nearest and dearest into the care of someone at a very emotional time, it is a very real concern as to how they will be treated.

Curious, I wanted to be able to give the families a satisfactory explanation, so I decided that I would make further investigations. As the inevitability of death forms a significant part of a District Nurse's role, I was keen to undergo any training that would serve to enhance my skills in this area. An aptly entitled course, 'Care of the Dying', was advertised, and with the help and encouragement of my then manager, I applied for a place on the course and was accepted.

The course, as part of its practical element, encouraged students to spend time in an area associated with the subject. A hospice and specialist cancer care centres and clinics were described as offering suitable opportunities to spend time with experts in palliative care. While I am no expert in palliative care, I did have a reasonable grasp of what questions the patients and the members of their families may direct at me, and I had decided that my particular area of weakness was in the care after death. When asked where I would like to conduct my placement I explained the reasoning behind my choice. Interestingly, the response among my peers and the course tutors was mixed, with some feeling it was not really pertinent and others agreeing that this was a great idea.

I was very surprised that my request was the first of its kind, and, as such, I had little guidance as to where to find a willing funeral director. Fortunately, this proved to not be as difficult a feat as I had imagined. There is an old Bhuddist proverb that states 'When the student is ready, the teacher appears,' and the ideal opportunity was to present itself bang on cue.

Oxley's funeral services was a long-established family firm, set up and run initially by Bill and Doris and later joined by their sons and now the latest generation of the family. They dissipated any images of the 'cold' undertaker. They were friendly to me, and they were known locally for their warmth and humour. They possessed an ability to offer incredible humility and genuine concern during difficult circumstances without appearing false and dispassionate.

Bill and Doris had set up the business from scratch with Bill starting his working life initially as a stonemason. It may seem odd to say that this family's business was a labour of love, but it was obvious to see how much love went into each role within the company—from the stone masonry to the one-to-one discussions regarding the wishes of the family. Each area was treated with the same professional, compassionate manner.

During my week spent with the team I was to witness the intricacies of life in the funeral world. I was fortunate to experience all aspects of this little known trade, including choosing and lining a coffin, laying out the body, caring for the deceased, assisting and supporting during viewing, and conducting a funeral, a burial, and a cremation. What impressed me was the way that each funeral was totally unique and how individual wishes were accounted for.

As in life so in death we are a nation of very different people. One of the essential aspects to working on a daily basis with such intense emotions is to be able to see the lighter side of life. In common with the health professions, it is necessary to have a smile and a giggle when appropriate. While maintaining professional conduct, we are first and foremost human beings, and, as such, humour is a big part of our collective lives. One such occasion the team chose to share with me involved managing a very delicate situation.

Following the death of an elderly gentleman the preparation prior to the funeral followed its usual course without any hitches, that is, until a frantic phone call from the wife of the deceased on the morning of the burial. The lady had discovered while preparing for the funeral that her false teeth did not fit. She explained that during the days since her husband's death she had not worn her teeth. The set of teeth she had sent to the funeral home were indeed her set, and there could be no prizes for guessing where they now were. Fortunately, the lady saw the funny side of what could have been a difficult situation, and she was reunited with the rightful set of teeth, and her husband was buried with his.

My time spent with the team presented a steep learning curve, as I witnessed the expert demonstration of preparation of the deceased prior to burial or cremation. Delivering the eulogy forms a significant part of the undertaker's duties. Deciding what is to be said about a whole life when it has to be a summary delivered in a few minutes is by no means an easy task. During a lifetime we all experience life-changing events, highs, lows, moments of brilliance, and moments we would rather forget. These events come together to form an incredible tapestry, and to tell that story to a captive audience requires a great deal of skill. To watch a well-delivered eulogy is to witness an amazing tribute to the deceased. I was fortunate to see a master craftsmen conduct several memorable services during my week.

Bill, as head of the family, had an intuitive way of saying the right things at the right time, and his ability to bring humour to an otherwise tense situation was a pleasure to watch. A modest and respectful man, Bill's years of life experience were demonstrated in his approach, achieving the appropriate balance between a person's religious/spiritual needs and their history, brought to life in a way that demonstrated with incredible detail and precision that happy times were had. It is uncanny how many of us remember vividly what we hear and learn about a person at their funeral.

It therefore seemed a fitting tribute that upon Bill's death his eulogy was delivered principally by those who knew and worked with Bill over many years. It was an amazing testament to this incredible man that his own apprentice of numerous years led the service that held the packed crematorium in a state of awe. I felt certain as I drifted out of the building that Bill would have emphatically agreed that his life's work had not been wasted, and he could indeed rest in peace knowing that his teachings had been passed on to the next generation of the family business.

CHAPTER 7

A maggot of distinction

I remember as a teenager believing that I was truly part of a new generation discovering trends that were brand new and unique to me and my contemporaries. It was a belief that was to be dispelled upon hearing from my parents comments like 'Nothing in history is new', 'Everything eventually comes back into fashion', and 'We wore those.' Discovering at the time that fingerless gloves, leg warmers, and stilettoes were nothing new was a revelation to an emerging fashion victim. I did not know then that I was to discover that fashion not only exists in clothes and shoes but that it extends to custom and practice in professions.

A classic example that has witnessed many changes in nursing is 'moving and handling'. Historically known to many as 'manual handling', this once acceptable practice is now viewed with virtual contempt and judgement by anyone associated with Health and Safety. I know words are powerful, but to accidently replace the word *manual* with *moving* you would think that you have seriously blasphemed. Hushed profuse apologies, and red faces usually accompany such a misdemeanour. Even worse than this, however, are the 'lifts' that were used and later banned by Health and Safety because of being deemed totally unsuitable and risky for both nurse and patient.

Ask any nurse who has been in the profession for approximately twenty years or more about the 'Australian Lift', and I am betting that despite possibly having paid the ultimate price by having ongoing lower back pain, he or she will get very animated and will declare excitedly that it was the best lift ever. 'The patient practically flew up the bed.'

Another area that has experienced changes and that has then returned to previously relegated treatments is wound care. No matter how hard we try to dress up the benefits of larvae therapy, as soon as we start using the patient's own language, that is, 'maggots', even the most experimental and adventurous aren`t overly thrilled about sharing themselves with all things wriggling.

Larvae therapy had long been out of vogue in modern wound care, and so when a research laboratory in Bridgend, South Wales, championed the return of the 'maggot' I thought it would be useful for some of our patients who were not responding to more conventional treatment.

Persuading my boss at the time that the once shunned trusty maggot was indeed making a welcome return to wound care was not an easy bridge to cross. The new, super-improved, maggot was grown under sterile conditions in a laboratory, and it was not of the more well-known variety of blue bottle, but they were rather resplendent green bottles. These were the crème de la crème, football Premiership lot.

With funds limited, this was a decision that needed careful consideration with a sense of humour thrown in. What now has regained its rightful place as a very useful wound treatment was at that time yet to be widely available without considerable organisation. Having a reputation as a maggot trailblazer, news spread quickly among the surgery staff. Was it the cringe factor or was it a genuine interest in wound care? I suspect it was the cringe factor and natural curiosity that motivated the masses.

Finally getting the nod from my amazingly trusting boss, Kath, all was in place for our first adventure. Deciding on the patient was not as easy as it sounds. With any new treatment there is always some trepidation about being the 'guinea pig', but when that treatment involves something live there is another element to the decision. Long-standing wounds often discharge offensively smelling exudate, causing considerable embarrassment and often extreme pain. This combination of symptoms can lead to low mood and often social isolation for the patient.

Ida was a perfect example of the aforementioned. What on first examination appeared to be a small wound on her big toe was in fact of substantial depth, and a considerable amount of dead tissue meant that other than surgically removing the toe, we had exhausted all other options. The wound was long standing, and it had become extremely difficult for Ida to walk more than a few steps. It is a measure of how desperate some patients can become that what under normal circumstances would seem to be appalling becomes acceptable.

Agreeing to the treatment involved Ida trusting my judgement, and this highlights how significant it is to have a solid nurse-patient relationship based on mutual respect and trust. Understandably, Ida was concerned about confidentiality, and she did not want anyone outside of her immediate family knowing about the nature of her treatment. It cannot be underestimated how frightened Ida was: 'How many will there be? What if they eat my good tissue? Will I feel them? Will it hurt? Can they get out?'

Her queries were all rooted in very real concerns, and they were ones that I too would have wanted answers to before sharing my bed with a crowd of 'maggots'. The day finally arrived and I am not sure who was the most nervous, Ida, myself, or the larvae. The patient's GP, Barrie, as well as some nursing colleagues had requested to be present.

I had visited the lab in Bridgend, and thus I was aware and prepared for the application. I think it was somewhat of a disappointment when I revealed the larvae from the small, sterile container in which they had been shipped. Everyone appeared to be holding his or her breath in anticipation of our larvae appearing, only to be slightly disappointed when out of the tube appeared miniscule larvae that were dispersed onto the toe before secure net dressings were applied to contain them. 'Is that it?' asked Barrie.

'Yes, that's it now, for three days.'

The drama of the treatment had not lived up to its billing, and to say that my audience considered it all a big anti-climax was not an exaggeration. I think this confirms how our own thoughts considerably shape our expectations. It was as if we were awaiting these huge larvae with enormous teeth that would make us all want to run to the hills with fear. As the crowd quickly dispersed because of their obvious lack of interest, I was left to write up my notes, with a much relieved and calmer patient.

Three days later, and I returned to remove the dressings. Needless to say, the initial excitement had evaporated at the surgery, and what had been the topic of conversation among the staff had been very much relegated to yesterday's news. In my naivety I was totally unprepared for what awaited me under the dressings. The drama was still to play out, as devouring the dead tissue had increased the size of the larvae dramatically, and I found myself in a state of shock.

While thrilled that they had accomplished their mission, I nearly dropped the dressing complete with the wrigglers. It is extremely rare for me to be lost for words, but this was one of those occasions. I wondered what the patient would think if she happened to see the size of the creatures that had been inside her dressing. I imagined that she would be totally horrified.

Desperately trying to appear calm and collected, I somehow upturned the dressing and contents into the clinical waste bag and expertly turned in a single spin to deposit the bag and its contents onto the patient's coal fire. It was with huge relief but somewhat of a conscience that I watched the 'Welsh giants' end their days as they were incinerated.

The splendid news was that the difference to the wound was dramatic, and I was amazed that in such a short time so much dead tissue had disappeared. Another couple of treatments later, and the wound was clean and healthy, going on to heal after a few more weeks. It is not an understatement to say that Ida's life was totally transformed. Pain, odour, isolation, restricted mobility, low mood, and insomnia became a distant memory—all thanks to a patient overcoming negative thought patterns and investing her trust in other people.

Being open to change in treatments and responding to the needs of our patients is both essential and a challenge, but, as this case demonstrates, the results far outweigh the 'cringe factor'.

CHAPTER 8

An unsung hero

Occasionally we meet people in life who are not just extraordinary but who are without doubt 'unsung heroes'. Without such remarkable characters the NHS could not cope with the modern-day realities of caring for someone in his or her own home. The 'Wilfs' of this world are the unpaid heroes, who day in, day out continue to care for their loved ones under the most challenging of circumstances. They ask for little or no recognition of their contribution, and they are often overwhelmed when any attention is paid to them and particularly if praise is bestowed upon them.

Wilf and Barbara were born and raised only a few miles apart, and they and their families were part of their local community. Wilf and his only sibling, Edward, were born into a farming family, and both experienced the realities of life on a farm before the introduction of modern machinery. Ploughing, harvesting, and haymaking were tough, arduous tasks and there was little, if any, time for holidays and days off.

Like many couples of the same generation, Wilf and Barbara were childhood sweethearts, and on Wilf's twenty-first birthday the couple married and set up home in the village. Wilf carried on working for his family on the farm, and Barbara worked as a seamstress in the nearest town. Life was challenging and hard work, but both Wilf and Barbara had been brought up with a strong work ethic, and they enjoyed the challenges of their life together. Three children were to follow over the years, and when Barbara gave up paid employment to become a full-time housewife and mother the couple continued with their individual roles within their family unit. As Wilf explained to me, they adopted traditional family roles, and as a family they found this to suit their requirements.

For much of their lives both were of good health generally, so it came as a huge shock to the pair when Barbara was diagnosed with an extremely rare and life-threatening illness that has a significant affect on the nervous system. Initially, repeated falling was the main presentation of the illness, but this was to be quickly followed by loss of grip and slurred speech. In a relatively short period of time their lives were to change dramatically. Wilf—in his mid-fifties—even confessed that he had never washed or dried a dish in his married life. The kitchen was unknown territory, and he did not relish the thought of becoming intimately acquainted with its delights, and in such daunting circumstances, he was being given precious little time to adapt to the situation.

Acknowledging the likely progression of Barbara's disease required the couple to adapt to what was likely to be the challenging nature of their future; holidays were hastily booked, and the dreams that they had planned for their retirement were brought forward, as the race against time was in full swing.

On meeting the couple for the first time, I was immediately greeted by them both as 'one of the family'. At this stage of Barbara's illness she was virtually fully wheelchair-bound, and her speech was largely incoherent, apart from the occasional decipherable word. I had been informed by the previous District Nurse that Wilf had given up work to be Barbara's full-time carer, and apart from spasmodic family support from his children and a once-weekly, three-hour visit from a care agency, Wilf single-handedly provided the care. This involved toileting, bathing, feeding, and any other care that Barbara required. For even the most experienced of carers or nurses this would have felt itself to have been a huge commitment, but, for Wilf, who by his own admission 'was an outside man', this was quite remarkable.

Wilf is a self-confessed perfectionist, and he became an excellent self-taught cook. His fruit pies, cakes, and roast dinners were without doubt the most delicious that I have ever tasted. Not satisfied with these culinary delights, he decided to try his hand at baking Christmas cakes. His motivation here concerned not only perfecting his craft but was to do with Wilf demonstrating his generosity. Unable to leave the house, he decided that rather than shop for a Christmas gift for the staff at the medical practice he would make us a cake. It was extremely humbling that Wilf wanted to communicate his thanks to us, and over the years his cakes became legendary.

On my thirtieth birthday I wasn't surprised when he presented me with a cake in celebration. However, I certainly had not prepared myself for the female mud-wrestling scene that adorned the top. The intricate details of the two competitors made for a scene to behold, and it was pointed out to me which competitor was supposed to represent me.

When I brought to Wilf's attention that one of my breasts, depicted in icing, was significantly bigger than the other he jokingly replied that that is how the artist had viewed things. I think they call it artistic licence!

When GP Barrie celebrated his fiftieth birthday, I couldn't wait to witness Wilf's artistic impression of my follicly challenged colleague. Barrie's cake was equally impressive, but it lacked the intimate detail that had been part of mine. A stethoscope, a doctor's bag, and a prescription pad crafted in icing sugar were no competition for a 'mud-wrestling nurse'. Such was the tradition that, for several years, and even after the death of Barbara, Wilf continued to provide us with our wonderful Christmas cake and, as Christmas approached, the staff would eagerly await delivery of the masterpiece.

When Barbara's condition worsened, her inability to swallow dictated that she had to be fed artificially by a tube leading directly to the stomach. Wilf negotiated if this could be carried out overnight so that he could continue to take Barbara out during the day. This was agreed, and Wilf was delighted that he could continue to visit the local indoor water park leisure complex. There are well-known benefits of hydrotherapy for people suffering from conditions that cause extremely painful spasms, and so Wilf and Barbara were regular visitors to the establishment.

It is a rarity to witness between two people the loving devotion that this couple demonstrated, particularly at a time when divorce rates have reached an all-time high, stress being frequently cited as the cause of marital breakdown. Wilf would, with the help of a carer, carry and lift Barbara into the whirlpool. It was obvious from the smiles and the spontaneous laughter that the stimulation from the warm water and the contact with caring lifeguards provided the couple with a welcome interlude from the constant challenges that they endured. I'm sure that as well as the physical benefits, the psychological boost was invaluable.

The enormity of a life-changing condition on both carer and patient cannot be underestimated. The overall health and well-being of the carer is obviously critical. Wilf confessed that without his 'fags and tipple' he felt that he would not have been able to function. While Health Education is an important part of a nurse's role, it has to be balanced against the overall benefits of suggesting particular lifestyle choices in each situation. To lecture Wilf regarding the consequences of smoking would have served no purpose. It could be argued that without his two vices, Wilf's emotional and psychological health would have suffered significantly.

To lose Barbara to such an aggressive and unforgiving illness was devastating enough for Wilf, but further tragedy was to follow, as the disorder was hereditary, and Diana, the couple's eldest daughter, went on to develop it. As a senior nursing sister, and having witnessed her mum's decline, she knew only too well what fate awaited her. It is well documented that, when questioned, parents unanimously proclaim that the worst thing that could happen to them is for their child to die before them. For Wilf, now in his mid-seventies, to witness the deterioration in Diana's health was without question the most painful experience of his life.

Diana led an exceptionally private life; her companions and soulmates were her dog and her cats. Forced to finish her nursing career because of her rapidly declining health, Diana recognised that she would need to give up her home in the East of England and return to the North West to be closer to her father and siblings. This shy and often blunt young woman was, by definition, a loner, and in many respects she was not at all comfortable spending time with others.

My first meeting with Diana some years earlier was memorable to say the least. I remember one of my nursing staff pre-warning me the day that I was to meet Diana and advising that I should not take things personally. Wanting to form my own opinion and not pre-judge the lady, I was determined to meet and greet Diana with a friendly and open manner.

'Who has parked in my space?' were her first words to me.

'Hi. You must be Diana?' I replied, wearing my friendliest of smiles. It had no effect whatsoever.

'Shift your car now.'

It was much like a trusting and faithful hound who does not know when 'it is time to quit' that I tried again. I offered sincere apologies regarding the car's offending position and moved it off the drive before diving in again with, 'Your Mum and Dad have told me so much about you; it's great to finally meet you.' Diana looked away.

I was to discover with time that Diana never made eye contact and was uncomfortable with doing so. Being a tactile person who also likes to make eye contact, I quickly learnt that the former was also a no-go area with Diana. Wilf explained to me that Diana had never hugged or kissed him or Barbara, and he had never seen her display any affection on any occasion. What remained a mystery to the family was why this painfully shy and reserved young woman had wanted to become a nurse from tender years in her childhood.

My hope was that engaging Diana on subjects that were closer to her heart would be the best way forward with our faltering relationship. Rescue dogs, nursing, gardening, and tennis provided the beginnings of a tentative bridge for the future. It never ceases to amaze me that however shy someone may be if you find a topic that he or she is passionate about then the previous boundaries can melt away relatively easily. I was to discover over time that this brave lady, despite never being openly friendly, had a great depth to her.

Our job as nurses is to ultimately respect each patient for who they are. Part of the care plan that we create with the patient should be based upon the uniqueness of his or her personality. The challenge that we all encounter in a diverse world is accepting that as individuals we will discover new and sometimes challenging traits in others that we have never before come across. It is said that we come into one another's lives for 'a reason or a season', and in the case of Wilf and Diana this was definitely true.

Breaking off a long-standing relationship with a family following the death of a patient is not to be done without attention and planning. For the District Nurse and carers it is often a tricky dilemma to work out how to withdraw from a remaining elderly spouse. Having been a daily or sometimes four-times-daily visitor to the home, it is a harsh reality of the care system that we do not have the facility to withdraw slowly in order to ease the drastic change.

My own personal experience has taught me that we intuitively sense when the time feels right, and that this only comes with years of experience. It is an area of care that does not receive any funding, and I feel it can be a difficult and sometimes complex process.

With target-led healthcare it is impossible to input into the system the visiting of bereaved spouses, and including these patients in our modern, computer-generated, face-to-face contacts is a nigh impossibility.

There is obviously a facility to conduct an initial bereavement visit, but it is typically an event that takes place in the nurse's own time. In the rare case of Wilf, we were, and we remain to this day, friends. Exceptional circumstances generate exceptional friendships, and having gone on to nurse Diana in her own home, with Wilf and daughter Helen shouldering the load, it came as no surprise that I was the nurse on duty the night that she died. It was my responsibility to visit the family and confirm that Diana had died. The irony was not wasted on any of us.

During the last few months of Diana's life I would sit and read short stories to her from the acclaimed *Chicken Soup for the Soul* series of books. The choice was often heart-warming tales of dogs and cats, and we sat in companionable silence, with happy tears rolling down our cheeks.

It is one of the greatest privileges to be asked to write and read the eulogy at the end of someone's life, and I felt honoured when Helen, along with Wilf and his son, John, asked me to carry out this tribute.

When a life appears to have been 'cut short', according to our cultural expectations, we can easily be drawn into what this untimely death has robbed us of. A different perspective, however, is to focus on what a life has offered and to think of the amazing impact that the life had on others. Diana's contribution to her patients, colleagues, family members, neighbours, and pets was considerable, and this was reflected in the tribute and in the celebration of her life. For Wilf, this recognition was an essential part of his grieving, and it provided some comfort in the early part of this process.

I have mentioned before how I no longer believe in coincidences, and I am instead truly convinced that, as cases like this one demonstrate, we were always destined to share in one another's lives.

Given the facts and how they played out I wonder what you the reader conclude from this particular example.

CHAPTER 9

The Queen of hearts

Whether or not to accept gifts that are offered as a token of a patient's gratitude presents a difficult dilemma to the nurse, as our code of professional conduct makes it perfectly clear that we should not receive such offerings under any circumstances. I have lost track of the times that I have offended patients and their loved ones by politely refusing their gestures of good will. Despite my code of conduct I have to admit that on occasions I have chosen, as have many of my colleagues, to accept the customary box of chocolates or bottle of wine when it has been brought to the surgery with a thank-you card. Patients find it difficult to express and quantify their gratitude any other way, and I feel it can do more harm to continuously rebuff their wishes.

One of the consequences of working in a rural area is the never-ending supply of whatever types of fruit and vegetable happen to be in season. I have had the privilege to sample some of the most delicious tomatoes, potatoes, and damsons, and I vividly remember being given a prize-winning marrow by an elderly farmer. Nice as it was, there is a limit to what one can do with a marrow. I doubt anyone ate as much marrow in the entire universe that week as I did. Stuffed, curried, fried, and boiled—you name it, I tried it that week. I think the sheer size of it would have fed the whole village.

Another unusual gift bestowed on me was from Iris, the widow of an eighty year-old GP. I had been instructed to regularly monitor this lady's blood pressure, as it was persistently high despite various attempts at controlling it with medication. The lady, similar to many people with hypertension, had no symptoms, and she subsequently had succumbed to a couple of small strokes.

A proud Irish lady, Iris had moved to England to accompany her husband, who was a GP for many years before he had died following a long battle with cancer. Iris had a very strong Irish brogue and a really cracking sense of humour; we shared our latest jokes during my visits, and we would often end up with tears rolling down our cheeks as laughter enveloped us both.

I had been a regular visitor during a period of approximately one month when Iris started to share with me some quite personal family insights. Iris strongly suspected that her only daughter, who lived a short distance away, was somewhat embarrassed by Iris's behaviour, but she explained to me that she had every intention of growing old disgracefully. She had made a promise to her husband that she would continue to have fun for as long as she was able. Iris enjoyed alcohol, and she was often to be seen having a glass of wine or sherry or a gin and tonic during the day.

It was on one of these occasions when she perhaps felt somewhat relaxed in my company that she handed me a brown paper bag and asked me if I would accept this small gift from her. As usual, I launched into my well-rehearsed explanation of why we were unable to accept gifts. It was obvious by her reaction that this statement caused considerable distress. 'But you must,' she said, 'I can't keep it here any longer in case my daughter finds it.'

'Why would that matter?' I asked.

The explanation that followed had me splitting my sides with laughter. Iris revealed that the previous year she had visited Amsterdam on a coach trip with a small group of her elderly female friends, and while walking around the red light district she had gone into a sex shop and, for fun, had bought a pack of playing cards. Now these cards were not your average pack; the cards were a graphic display of fifty-two different sexual positions, each card depicting a naked male and female. They apparently left nothing to the imagination. My own imagination ran riot, as I visualised the tabloid headings: 'Nurse sexually corrupted by elderly patient'.

Between the two of us we came up with many more possibilities for these headlines, some too near the knuckle to share within this text. Eventually we reached the sensible decision that to destroy the evidence before it caused any future rise in both of our blood pressures was the most adult solution. The next concern was whether anyone would examine the contents of her dustbin.

It was decided that I would dispose of the evidence on my return to the surgery, in the waste bin located there. I am sure that never before has the disposal of a pack of playing cards needed so much careful and precise planning. On my return to the surgery, during a coffee break, I had great fun sharing my story with our senior GP Barrie.

Zoë: 'I have an unusual request. Do you have any objections if I dispose of something less than customary in our paper shredding bag?'

Barrie: 'Well it depends on what it is.'

Zoë: 'I think it's easier if I show you.'

Barrie: 'Where the hell have you had those from?'

Zoë: 'That's a patient confidentiality issue.'

Barrie: 'Come on—give us a clue.'

Zoë: 'Irish. Full of mischief. Member of the fairer sex. Of advancing years.'

Barrie: 'Enough said. No problems. Leave them with me, and I will destroy the evidence.'

Zoë: 'Not a chance. With your memory lapses, they will probably appear in someone's notes!'

The truth was that I felt that the continued curiosity of my male colleague may get the better of him, and I wasn't going to take any chances at this stage; I, like my patient, needed to sleep soundly in my bed. The weight of responsibility weighed heavily on my conscience, and never before had the process of shredding felt so satisfying. After the deed was done I was able to ring the patient to relate that it was a case of 'mission accomplished'. Interestingly, despite not having any direct proof of the cause, the patient's blood pressure reduced significantly after this, and I also stopped having sleepless nights!

As my time visiting Iris concluded we both realised that the secret we had shared had in some ways cemented our nurse-patient relationship in a most unique way. What it did demonstrate to me, while not perhaps conventional in the obvious sense, was the level of trust that patients place in their nurse.

CHAPTER 10

Loss of manhood

My role as the District Nurse in a rural village meant that I was a regular visitor to the local farms, and over time I learnt that there is little place for sentimentality while trying to maintain a business that is fraught with European Union laws and declining milk yields. I am pleased to report that my experiences of the farms that I visited were positive, and I saw generations of farmers trying to keep their proud heritage alive. During the outbreak of foot and mouth in 2001 I witnessed the devastation that this caused as herds were slaughtered.

The alarming rates of male suicide in farming communities is not surprising given the pressures that many find themselves under. I remember vividly how the suicide of a young local farmer devastated his family and the local community. Not known for their readiness to share their feelings, farmers often have virtually no medical notes, and, for that reason, when a member of this group actually visits their local GP or requests a visit, alarm bells should ring.

I have lost count of the amount of times that I have conducted an impromptu examination on a farmer in the yard or in one of a number of farming outbuildings and confirmed a farmer's suspicions regarding, among other things, hernias, gangrenous toes in ill-fitting wellington boots, urine infections, and, on one occasion, a sexually transmitted infection. A nice, clean, and warm treatment room is obviously the most appropriate place to conduct any examination, but on such occasions if Mohammed won't come to the mountain then, as the saying goes, the mountain must come to Mohammed. ''ere, nurse, would you have a quick look at this?' is often the cue to a needy examination.

Many of the older farmers trusted me to see parts of their anatomy that remained mystical to their own wives. Bill was such a man. A farmer all of his adult life, he had been a virtual stranger to the medical profession until a diagnosis of diabetes in his later years. Big in every way, he was not only largely built but otherwise someone with a huge presence—'one of life's characters' as they say. His tales of the past were very enthralling and often hilarious. He loved being the centre of attention, and over the years I noticed that he did exercise some poetic licence while maintaining the general thread of the story.

Trust among these patients is built up only over time, and in the case of Bill, because of the embarrassing nature of the problem, he had, in his words, 'doctored things me self, nurse, with TCP lotion'. On revealing the cause of his concerns, it was not difficult to assume that this was not a new problem. As well as visual clues to an illness, very often the odour confirms our suspicions that all is not well.

I remember when undergoing some training with a GP that he commented, 'Common things are common, and rare things are rare.' Naturally, in the majority of cases, this was indeed good advice. However, in a full nursing career we will sometimes stumble upon these rare conditions, and in Bill's case this was so. For a gentleman of Bill's generation it is virtually unheard of to willingly expose one's 'manhood' to a young nurse, so I knew only too well that this was something of serious concern to him. Fortunately, a nurse knows from experience that no matter how shocking an illness presents itself to the eye, we should always be acutely aware that the patient is more than likely to be carefully watching for our reaction, and it is therefore essential not to reveal our horror. There are occasions when this is indeed a severe test, and this was one of those such occasions.

Cancer of the penis is rare, and in nearly thirty years of nursing I have only witnessed it twice. Bill admitted that he had been self-treating himself for several months, and this was evident by the progression of his symptoms. It was a matter of urgency that Bill be admitted to hospital for surgery.

Persuading an elderly farmer who has rarely left his village and who has certainly not done so previously for medical reasons, to go into hospital for surgery, almost without doubt to have his penis amputated, is not an everyday occurrence, and there is no easy way or textbook description to break this kind of news. Winning the trust of a patient in these circumstances is a finely balanced situation. One wrong word can be the difference between life and death— literally. Knowing the patient and using his or her language patterns when relating the news—even if they are not perhaps those that we are accustomed to—can make all the difference.

'Will the old lad have to come off, Sister?' was Bill's way of tackling the difficult subject matter.

'Yes. There is a strong possibility that this might be the case,' was the most honest response I could give.

'How will I pee?'

This was a very reasonable question to ask, under the circumstances. Likening the operation to that of a transgender reconstruction was not I felt going to be of assistance, and so explaining that there would be an opening made underneath seemed straightforward and practical and an acceptable response for Bill. 'That's OK. It's not as if I need it for anything else—them days are behind me, Nurse. I had me moments, mind. I used to be known as The Bull!' This brief and light-hearted reference we both realised was his acknowledgement that in terms of his sexual prowess the surgery would end any opportunity of a future sex life.

That half an hour of straight talking made all the difference to this frightened, elderly man, who went on to have a successful operation and, following a short period of wound dressings, went on to live a fulfilled life, minus 'the old lad'. Interestingly, he confided that he never looked 'down there' following the surgery. It would be wrong to assume that because of Bill's advanced years the change of body image would not have had an effect on his life. This operation probably caused incredible distress, both psychologically and emotionally.

When a woman loses a breast, it is universally accepted and understood that this can often result in the female feeling a loss of her sexuality. While discussing issues around sexuality is not always an easy topic, particularly if in discussion with the opposite sex and a member of an older generation, it is essential that we don't dismiss this very important matter. In Bill's situation he chose to introduce the subject masked with humour, but it presented an opening for discussion. Sexuality and intimacy for some patients in their twilight years forms a very important part of their lives, and the challenge facing the nurse is to skilfully approach the subject with respect and care.

As mentioned earlier, Bill adapted to his new situation very well, and he displayed no obvious embarrassment. On more than one occasion I witnessed him discussing his new 'waterworks' with guests. His tendency to exaggerate had some of his elderly male contemporaries wincing with pain and begging him to 'shut up'.

One of my abiding memories of Bill was a conversation I overheard where one of his, shall we say, braver and more curious, pals, asked, 'What does it look like down there?'

'I have no idea,' was the response.

'How come?'

'Because I've never looked down there. 'If I can't see it then I can choose to remember things as they were.'

This to me signified that despite his bravado this courageous old farmer was naturally affected by his radical bodily change but had managed to cope by using his usual tendency to bring humour to a situation.

CHAPTER 11

Things that go bump in the night

Some topics create controversy and divide opinion. One such area fraught with debate is around all things supernatural. I, as many of my colleagues, have been drawn into debate with our patients over shared experiences. One such episode that springs to mind was regarding the alleged haunted home of an elderly lady who was close to death.

We had been asked to provide some overnight nursing care to allow this lady's wish to die at home to be fulfilled. As so many people's preferred place to end their life is in their own home, it is quite common during the last few days of life to provide a nurse to carry out nursing care during the night. This allows the family to catch up with rest /sleep and enables them to be able to cope with the intense needs of the terminally ill patient. In the majority of cases the family/loved ones remain in the home and are reassured that they will be woken if the situation worsens. On this occasion the lady's only living relative, her nephew lived a substantial distance away. A close friend was her main support, and she lived locally. The patient's friend was to provide us with access to the house.

Even for those of us who are sceptical of haunted house stories, it would be hard not to fall under the spell of this property. My first impressions, after leaving the main road, were of an extremely creepy, dilapidated, large, detached home, in substantial, unlit, grounds. The date, illuminated by my torch over the door, identified it as a Tudor property. Thoughts of creepy *Scooby-Doo*-type houses sprung to mind, and it would not have surprised me if I had seen Yvette Fielding of the popular British paranormal mystery TV series *Most Haunted* appear out of the darkness.

As I stood awaiting access to the house in the pitch black, I experienced that bodily sensation that is most accurately described as 'being scared stiff'. Not one to normally be spooked by ghostly tales, I became all too aware that I was becoming hypersensitive, and the old 'fight or flight' response was swinging into full working operation.

Picture the scene: a large heavy oak door with accompanying heavy metal door knocker that would not have looked out of place at a stately home. As is often the case in these situations, the wind and rain were doing their best to throw me off my feet, and so the accompanying shivering and chattering teeth only added to the picture of a very scared District Nurse, definitely out of her comfort zone. I remember that my apprehension was off the scale as the heavy door swung open. A huge part of me was tempted to run off and pretend to my colleagues that I had not been able to gain access to the house, but the morally upstanding version of me won the ensuing debate, and I remained rooted to the spot, awaiting my fate.

One characteristic we share as human beings is that of immediately establishing first impressions of one another. It is inherent in us all to quickly form an opinion of that which we see, hear, feel, and so forth. On this occasion I was already on edge with the increasing amount of adrenaline and cortisol I was releasing. The effect of this huge surge of hormones had the usual effects on my gut and bladder, and I was in serious need of locating the toilet promptly. Initial introductions were exchanged, and I was invited in. As the heavy door was shut behind me, it would not have seemed out of place for the accompanying hinges to have creaked loudly, adding to the already creepy surroundings. As we proceeded to pick our way through the downstairs rooms, it quickly became obvious that the furnishings and decor were in keeping with the age of the house. Each room we entered was crammed with stuffed animals displayed in glass cabinets, of various sizes. It was a taxidermist's dream with a full range of assorted animals from weasels to cobras, and foxes to owls.

Wherever you looked, a pair of eyes appeared to be trained on you. I was beginning to understand how a field mouse must feel when under the scrutiny of a bird of prey. It was most disconcerting as the wattage of the bulbs was so low that you felt like you were entering a twilight world. In addition to my stiff companions, we were also surrounded by an equally creepy large collection of antique porcelain dolls. In failing light I would challenge anyone to not feel freaked out under these circumstances.

We eventually made our way up a creaking staircase, which led to a huge bedroom. Against one wall was the most majestic, dark oak, four-poster bed that I had ever seen. In the centre of this bed, which would have slept a family of four comfortably, lay a tiny figure that looked literally lost against the pillow. The once plush antique furniture and drapes had become faded and worn with time, and the air of neglect hung over the room like a cloud.

I was introduced to my patient by her friend. The patient was an elderly lady, and she was already in a deeply unconscious state. Her appearance was obviously important to her, but, unfortunately, her heavily made-up face, with thick, greasy, dark foundation and over-rouged cheeks gave her a look similar to one of her porcelain dolls. It appeared to have been on for some time, and it suggested that there was layer upon layer.

Sadly, her once crowning glory, a brunette wig, did little to enhance her complexion. As a consequence of her significant weight loss, the wig looked like it was lost against this tiny face, and it was perched at a strange angle that left you with a stiff neck. In any other circumstances the situation would have created a comedic scene, but at this time it was sad to witness. It created a dilemma in many respects, as the temptation was overwhelming to want to straighten the wig, but the danger was that doing so may make a bad matter worse. I therefore decided that for the time being the wig would remain out of bounds.

As I pulled up a chair by the side of this huge bed, I was struck by the distance that remained between me and my patient. All nurses have it drilled into us during our training that to sit on the bed of a patient significantly increases the risk of cross-infection, and it is a practice that is totally outlawed. As with most rules, from time to time there are occasions, dare we say, that common sense prevails, and in order to be physically closer to this dying patient I chose to clamber up on to this once majestic bed. The importance of physical closeness, particularly prior to death, outweighed any concerns I had regarding the risk of infection.

While intimate contact is reserved for those who know and love the patient, a hand held or a gentle brush of the skin is an essential way to let a patient know that we are there for them, physically as well as emotionally. Verbally communicating with patients who are unable to respond can be quite off-putting, but it is an essential part of the nurse's role to carry on treating the patient with the same courtesy that you would extend to any patient.

During the introduction period I had heard the front door knocker announce the arrival of my nurse colleague, Jackie, and within a short time she was shown up to the bedroom to join us. The unspoken word between nurses is often very useful in tense situations, and on this occasion our mutual look of terror was more than evident. Huge, dilated pupils and a slight tremor left me in no doubt that my colleague was indeed sharing the need to use the toilet.

Our mutual fear was to be multiplied tenfold when the patient's friend informed us that if we heard any sounds that resembled footsteps on the staircase, we were not to worry, as it was the ghost of a young maid who had committed suicide by hanging herself in the patient's bedroom. There are moments in all our lives when we truly aren't sure how to react to a situation; we are unsure whether to laugh or cry, and our reaction can be quite uncharacteristic.

Being placed in a responsible, professional position in this situation dictated my response, and I tried to appear calm and matter-of-fact about the comment, despite how I was actually feeling. For Jackie, however, it was, shall we say, the proverbial straw that broke the camel's back, and she was unable to contain her mounting fear. Totally petrified by what she had just been told, she sought immediate reassurance from our informant. 'You are joking, aren't you?'

'Definitely not,' was the serious response, said with an accompanying straight face. 'Most nights you hear her walking the stairs.'

Further comments regarding the ghost's restless search for peace did nothing to dampen down our fear. Uncharacteristically, but totally understandably, my colleague responded, 'There's no way I`m staying here on my own.'

My role was to ensure that both patient and nurse were settled before I left them over night so that I could visit other patients as the on-call sister for the night. Never before had this posed a problem, but by now it was more than obvious that I would not be able to leave Jackie alone. It was even doubtful that I would be able to honour my need for the toilet without her company! They say that nurses can multi-task, but I was perplexed as to how I could be in two places at once.

As time appeared to be quickly evaporating, I made the split decision that I would stay overnight with the nurse and patient. I imagined the interesting but challenging conversation that would take place in the morning with my then manager. The matter of budgetary constraints was a topic we were all more than aware of. Persuading managers that two nurses were needed because of ghostly goings-on would undoubtedly be a tall order, but at least it was one I would be facing in the relative safety of the daylight.

While I had made the decision to stay overnight, I would be lying to say that I was at ease with the situation. Following the departure of the patient's friend, my terrified colleague and I attempted to make light of the state of affairs by agreeing that the very 'British' way to deal with such a challenge would be to brew-up and keep calm! The problem with this solution was that with the exception of managing our toileting needs neither of us felt at all comfortable being left alone. With the tea poured and our bladders emptied, we were ready for the walk of doom past the staring eyes of assorted stuffed wildlife and pot dolls.

I felt it was highly likely that the contents of my tea cup would end up in the saucer as my trembling hands resembled someone who was suffering from severe alcohol withdrawal. Jackie and I took up our positions for the night sitting adjacent to the patient. To say we were hyper-vigilant would be an understatement. The slightest creak or groan had us both jumping up like scared rabbits in the headlights.

As the patient slept peacefully, our fragile states were not helped by the impromptu appearance of an elderly, frail cat, which made his entrance via the allegedly haunted staircase. I am sure that at some point in time the cat had been as resplendent as the now tired four-poster bed, but the ageing process had robbed our feline companion of his once lustrous white Persian coat, and in its place was what can only be described as a sad, dirty, grey, clumpy, and matted rug of a coat. Having only one eye completed the rather pathetic picture.

We were to later learn that the aptly named 'Snowy' was in fact old enough in cat years to have made our patient appear a mere teenager! The patient had expressed, as part of the instructions following her death, that her dear companion 'Snowy' was to be euthanised, and his ashes were to go in with that of the patient's. The friendship had been long and treasured, and it seemed somehow prophetic that the pair remained together following their deaths.

I have to admit that during that night of terror there was more than one occasion when Jackie and I came close to joining Snowy and our patient on the four-poster bed. It is said that as the 'fight or flight' mode kicks in, and when we are in a heightened state of alertness, our senses become finely tuned, and I can most definitely confirm this. I felt that, for one night only, my hearing rivaled that of a bat!

Anyone who regularly does night shifts will confirm that there is a certain time during their shift when they have a real battle to keep their eyes open, and there is a need to walk about in order to ward off succumbing to sleep. There was more chance of hell freezing over that night than of us being seduced into any slumbering. There was no need or wish to get up and walk about. It amazed me how quickly, given a creepy environment and a story to match, we become so easily drawn into the drama. We became totally time distorted with minutes appearing to last hours. What seemed to be a truly frightening environment to us was the patient's long-term family home, and where she felt secure. Her hobbies and interests of taxidermy and collecting Victorian pot dolls were obvious passions and loves, whereas for us, all it appeared to do was add to the creepiness of the place.

As daylight signalled that morning was approaching, we continued to sit on the bed, literally on the edge of our seats. The patient, however, appeared to remain totally peaceful as her time of death approached. Despite my dramatic poetic licence during this chapter I can assure you, the reader, that the patient's holistic needs were met. I wouldn't want my ever so slightly exaggerated description leaving you under the impression that the patient got more attention from Snowy!

An experience of this kind, however, makes a lasting impression on a nurse, and as we reflect back over a nursing career it is these distinct episodes that remind us of our responsibility to honour and celebrate the incredible diversities that exist. One of the most rewarding things about being a nurse for me is the fact that we are given an incredibly privileged opportunity to become acquainted with different races, cultures, and communities.

On the rare occasions that we may come face to face with something more diverse, as in this instance, we should embrace the challenge. There is always a silver lining in these extreme cases. Imagine how much lighter you will be after the experience.

CHAPTER 12

The mystery of the infected finger

Nurses and their medical colleagues like the rest of the general population find some patient behaviour offensive, and we occasionally have to 'bite our tongue' so to speak. We refer to these patients as heart-sinkers, for the obvious reason. A classic example of such a patient was Arthur.

The mere mention of Arthur's name in the surgery had us all wanting to run to the hills. Unkempt, this housebound elderly gentleman lived in what many would consider squalid conditions. I was to meet Arthur for the first time following a referral from one of the GP's. An infected finger was the source of the visit.

On my arrival to Arthur's home my gut feeling, which usually served me well, was screaming that this visit was going to be a test. What I was not prepared for was the magnitude of the test on all my senses. The exterior of the house was more than enough to cause concern. To describe it as dilapidated was to put it mildly. It was hard to believe that anyone was living inside. The brickwork was falling down; all the window and door frames appeared rotten, as were the external doors; and it had been many years since a paintbrush had made an appearance. The yard at the rear of the property was no stranger to litter, and the pervasive smell of rotting material did nothing to improve its overall impression. A deep breath and a positive internal voice willing me forward, gave me the strength to knock on the rotten door.

'Come in love,' signalled my invitation. If I thought my senses had been bombarded outside the property then I was underestimating the effect that the interior would take. All nurses know that over our career we develop a strong stomach. In much the same way as a celebrity model courts the camera, lights, and paparazzi, nurses court urine, vomit, faeces, and other bodily secretions. We become largely immune to the offensive odours of a rotting wound, and our nearest and dearest are amazed that we are able to relish our food immediately after dressing such a wound. We wear our strong stomach like a badge of honour. However, on this rare occasion, even my previously stoical stomach was to weaken under the pressure.

Following the voice through the filthy kitchen and into the main living area, I became quickly aware that Arthur shared his home with several cats. Cat litter trays were strategically placed throughout the house. All of the trays were in dire need of emptying, and the pervading odour of cat excrement was overwhelming. For the first time in my career I was unable to be discreet regarding my queasy stomach. Retching in front of a patient I had yet to introduce myself to was not customary, and I was mortified. I need not have worried, however, as from his chair my patient found the whole incident hilarious. Such an event would have horrified most people, but I was to find out that Arthur was not like most people. What would disgust many in fact appeared to appeal to this man. As I approached Arthur's chair it was obvious that his unkempt home extended to his appearance and level of hygiene. As he reached out his hand to me during our introduction, I was for once wishing that I had put on my gloves before greeting the patient. Extremely over-grown filthy fingernails and possibly the dirtiest hands I had ever seen were met with a reluctant handshake.

Following introductions, I was asked whether I was a cat lover. The feline population has done little to offend me over the years, but asking such a question under the particular conditions put my powers of reasoning to the test. 'I'm a dog person.'

Fortunately, Arthur seemed content with this response. 'I can't smell it meself nurse,' was his first reference to the contents of the cat litter. As we age naturally there is some decline in our senses, but the stench inside those four walls could have been detected by anyone with a nose!

After regaining my composure, the next obstacle to overcome was the proliferation of fleas that had decided to descend on the only tasty flesh available.

Arthur and the flea-ridden skinny felines were hardly any competition, and, as word travelled fast in the flea community, I was to become the main host for what appeared to be a whole flea generation. Young and old, they wasted no time in jumping on board. The assault on my nostrils paled into insignificance as intense itching now dominated my attention. It is indeed testament of a nurse's ability to multi-task when faced with the above situation that we can scratch while performing a sterile dressing without contaminating the patient. Rather than a direct scratch, we have to use the sharp edges of whatever presents itself in the environment—tables, chairs, walls, and so on.

In an attempt to try to tackle the problem of the obvious flea infestation I later contacted the local pest control department at the council. Arthur and his feline companions were no strangers to the pest control team. Previous visits had included treatment for rodent problems. Pet mice and rats I have no issue with, but the thought of mice and rats running riot during my visits filled me with dread. I was assured that the ever-present cats would almost certainly serve as a deterrent.

Arthur seemed oblivious to the flea invasion, as his attention was focused on his grossly infected finger, which he took great delight in introducing me to. I was informed that the original wound was sustained on a cat food tin, but it was now showing signs of infection and had become painful. Any infection of a digit is accompanied by pain and swelling, and it often becomes inflamed and discharges pus-like fluid. It was obvious that this septic finger would require regular dressings and a course of antibiotics. The initial challenge following obtaining a swab of the wound was where I could conduct the dressing.

There are rare occasions when it would seem more appropriate to clean your shoes on the way out of a house as opposed to before entering, and this was one of those times. Trying to find a bar of soap and a clean towel would have resulted in both the patient and me becoming fossilised, so I was extremely grateful that my nursing bag contained my antiseptic hand rub. It was the nearest I was going to get to maintaining some level of acceptable hygiene.

As I proceeded with the dressing I was to discover that Arthur's filthy condition extended to his language and to lewd suggestions regarding what he would like to do with me in his bedroom. During subsequent visits, and despite all attempts to deter these comments, he would profess to have the sexual energy of a man half his age. Our imagination tends to conjure up images of what we would like an elderly man to portray. An advert for Werther's Originals sweets, depicting a kindly grandfather figure, is a common representation. Unfortunately, what we tend to forget is that if a person has been sexually explicit in their younger days then it is unlikely that he will change in old age. Faced with what we consider to be unacceptable behaviour in the elderly, who are of sound mind, is a difficult area to manage.

Requesting that a patient in their eighties find a new GP practice in a rural area is fraught with difficulties. Morally, it is unfair to expect a neighbouring practice to accept the patient on to their books. Denying a patient the right to healthcare is a decision that no one in primary care is comfortable with. On this occasion, with the support of a listening ear from my GPs, I was able to carry on visiting for the duration of the treatment. I vividly remember on one occasion being early for a visit, and, as Arthur was still in bed, he called me through to the bedroom. My eyes streamed as a result of the ammonia fumes from his urine-soaked mattress and bedding. 'Get in with me, Nurse, and I'll show you what you're missing.' Not surprisingly, I wasn't wooed by the invitation. Interestingly, I was to find out that this widowed man had been unfaithful and physically and mentally abusive to his wife over many years, and as a result his numerous children no longer had any contact with him. He was a lonely, isolated man.

It is not for any of us to judge our patients, but as a human being first and foremost we have our own emotions to contend with, and I would be lying if I didn't admit to not liking this man. Among friends and family I am often referred to as 'Pollyanna', as I am an optimist, and I try to find good in everyone. I truly believe that there is the potential for good in us all. Trying to find any endearing features in Arthur, however, was literally like looking for the proverbial needle in what appeared to be a haystack of astronomical proportions. I was to discover from my social work colleagues that this elderly man's offensive behaviour and the filthy conditions in which he lived had resulted in a policy of only male care visits from the home care department. It was a sad state of affairs that Arthur's choice of behaviour had led to this drastic policy. Mutual respect and common courtesy form the basis of any relationship, and yet this was a fact that I had to reacquaint Arthur with at every visit. Pointing out to him that our shared intended outcome was to heal his infected finger, at times appeared totally wasted on him. The realities of a rare situation like this are that visits are conducted with a feeling of dread and a heavy heart. Interestingly, there is enough research to suggest that such visits over a protracted period can lead to a persistent negative mood for the nurse. I can confirm, purely on a personal note, that I have found this to be true. Fortunately, on this occasion, the visits only extended over a few weeks, but if the treatment had gone on for a longer period, we would have had to have given serious consideration to other options.

This particular case does, however, end on a humorous note. As I had suspected, the swab results confirmed that Arthur's finger was heavily infected. Fortunately, a course of powerful antibiotics and an appropriate dressing resulted in rapid improvement, and I was on the verge of discharging Arthur. It was in fact a total mystery when all progress halted, and there was in fact a deterioration of the wound. Mindful of the likelihood that Arthur was likely to get the dressing soiled, I always left it heavily bandaged. A further wound swab was obtained, and the results indicated that a new bacteria appeared to be causing the infection.

Unusually, I was not familiar with the reported bug. I decided to ring the pathology lab at the local hospital and discuss possible further treatment methods with the consultant microbiologist. I was told that it was an unusual bacterium, one normally to be seen in cat faeces.

'That explains a lot,' I replied.

After taking in this new information and armed with my thoughts, I headed off in search of an explanation from my patient. With the face of an innocent, cherubic child, Arthur denied all knowledge of how a heavily bandaged finger had become re-infected. I could smell a proverbial rat a mile off, and upon further questioning, and with some help from the home carer, I was made aware of the real cause of the problem. With a huge smile and a hearty laugh I found out that when Arthur thought that he was on his own he had removed the bandage and carefully rubbed his finger in some of the cat litter and then reapplied the bandage. Fortunately, his carer had caught him in the act that day and forced him to confess to the crime. A stern lecture regarding the cost to the NHS and the possible implications of his actions to his health were met with a feeble apology.

As mentioned more than once in previous chapters, this demonstrates in a rather alarming way how patients will go to extreme lengths to extend their care. The offending finger went on to heal over the next few weeks, and when the time came to cease visiting, Arthur presented me with a flowering geranium that he had grown from seed and invited me to call in any time I was passing for a cup of tea.

It will probably come as no surprise that I never took him up on his offer, but the gesture of the plant as a gift did remind me that underneath his offensive demeanour he did show on occasions a glimmer of acting like a decent human being. Arthur continued to live out his days alone in the same conditions.

After his death, the house was bulldozed to the ground, and in its place there was built a smart, residential property. It seems ironic that what was once an inhospitable house now resembled a bright new, stunning family home full of life.

CHAPTER 13

The magic of a gypsy angel

Without doubt, for many of us our greatest fear is ultimately death. The idioms around dying—'popping off', 'meeting our maker', 'shuffling off this mortal coil', 'kicking the bucket', 'passing over', 'passing away', and so forth—are numerous in our language as well as others, partly to help us deal with the subject. Ultimately, dying is the 'Daddy' of all fears, and, not surprisingly, it is a subject that has come up repeatedly during previous chapters. I, in keeping with the masses, share this very real fear, but I no longer do so to the extent that I once did. To be able to tell another that we don't harbour some fear about death is unusual but not unheard of.

The one thing that nursing provides us with is the very real opportunity to spend time with people as they approach death. In recent years, with the introduction of the Care Pathway in the UK—a plan to assist with symptom control at the end of life—we are now much more likely to discuss end-of-life care with a patient and his or her loved ones well in advance of his or her death. It is hardly a surprise that for a nation where maintaining control is practically a national obsession, the greatest test for many of us is to come to terms with the fact that we are unable to escape the end of our physical life.

We are largely a country, in keeping with many others, where the members are under the misconception that they have total control over their lives and the lives of others. Reassuring a loved one that he or she is not going to die is dishonest, and experience has taught me that, however well-intentioned the reassurance may be, this belief often results in pain and distress.

On a lighter note, if there was an international event on 'Maintaining Control', can you imagine the winner's rostrum? If entered as an Olympic event, we would triumph over the rest of the world. This isn't a knock at my fellow countrymen, but what it is instead is my attempt to bring some lightness and humour to a subject that we squirm with embarrassment about. The irony was not wasted on me during previous episodes of severe burnout.

Having to succumb and trust is our ultimate challenge, particularly for those of us without a strong religious belief. There are, however, times in life when the very act of taking a chance is all that we have left. Fear of the unknown for those who convince themselves that they have control is an extremely uncomfortable challenge. My belief is that we have somehow forgotten that death of the physical form is a normal part of life. Succeeding in my own challenge to let go and trust was ultimately a welcome relief from the chaos.

Like many, for a long while I truly convinced myself that I was on top of all things: friendships, family, paid work, voluntary work, planning holidays, caring for pets, and so forth. Letting go in any frightening situation, but particularly around death, requires courage. Where is the good news in all this? Well experience has demonstrated to me over the last thirty years that we are much more likely to be afraid of that which we feel is never discussed. As a child, being sent to another room at the mere hint of a discussion about death was common to a generation. Did it do any good? I doubt many would disagree that it did little to alley our mounting fears.

As a nurse, some deaths leave a lasting impression on us. An occasion that demonstrated to me that patients appear to transcend beyond their physical form when they cease living was the case of Donna Marie, a local young gypsy woman and the eldest of five sisters. Donna had been diagnosed as a child with a rare condition that affects kidney function and that causes growth retardation and anaemia, among several other symptoms. Donna was indeed a young woman of contrasts. Despite physically being of doll-like stature, her temperament was larger than life. Her singing voice was so powerful that she could make the hairs stand up on the back of your neck. Despite often feeling exhausted and unwell, Donna Marie was often at the heart of attempts to make life more bearable for others. Her great passion was raising funds for charity trips to support the work of Romanian orphanages. Donna's father, with other members of the gypsy and non-gypsy community, made several trips a year to distribute aid, and Donna was always planning supplies for the next mission. Donna's deep Christian belief was a huge comfort to her during the progression of her illness. She had become a born again Christian, and her devotion to her faith was virtually palpable. Her passion and gift to sing was experienced by many as she sang in various churches to raise funds.

As her impending death approached, she was often to be seen praying and reciting verses from the Bible. She also penned some amazingly moving words on the day prior to her death. Her faith allowed her to come to terms with her hastening demise, and she held hands with the GP and the nurses during our visits, verbalising that as death approached she was not afraid. During one of his last visits, her GP and my nursing colleague Julie were reduced to tears as she said a prayer for them.

In keeping with the gypsy tradition, funerals, and particularly those of a young person, draw huge crowds with people travelling in some cases hundreds of miles to pay their respects. Up to a thousand mourners attended, with many people having to listen from the grounds of the Bible College where the service took place. In accordance with Donna's wishes, she remained at her home for viewing and was later buried in a white nightgown laced with a beautiful lilac ribbon, which she had chosen. A white coffin was transported in a white hearse, and a traditional gospel choir sang at the graveside. The service was a mixture of modern and traditional, with all things in between.

Her GP and I were among those hand-picked by her family to contribute to the celebration of life. There are times in our lives when we put ourselves under extra pressure, as our need for things to go 'perfectly', because of the significance of the event, weigh heavily on our conscience. As my turn to speak grew ever closer I would not be lying when I say that my legs would not stop shaking. In keeping with many, I too was praying and asking God to help make this a memorable and worthy tribute to one of his greatest believers. I need not have worried, as my meticulously planned tribute appeared to hit the spot, so to speak. The rest of the service went equally well, and as the sun shone brightly, I felt that we collectively, as a diverse group of people, had paid tribute to Donna in a unique and fitting way.

During the weeks following the funeral I was to witness the grief of Donna's parents at it's rawest. As mentioned earlier, it comes as no surprise that when a parent is asked what they would consider to be their worst living nightmare, it is almost always reported to be their child dying before themselves.

Donna's grave was adorned with various mementoes, keepsakes, and tributes, and a bench was donated to the graveyard by the family. Jo, Donna's father would sometimes visit the grave several times a day. He was very uncomfortable with the thought that Donna was alone, and no amount of reassurance could help this grieving parent.

Most of us have experienced grief on some level, and for those of us that have, we know that it is not an emotion that can accurately be described by words. In the weeks immediately following a death, those left behind are often desperate for a sign that their loved one has passed on to another realm. Donna's heartbroken family, in keeping with this thought, were waiting for proof that she had made the transition.

Over the summer period that followed we enjoyed some prolonged sunny weather, and I would occasionally spend my lunch break on the bench next to Donna's grave. I found it a very calming and peaceful environment, and I felt at one with everything. During one of these visits, I remember comfortably chattering away to Donna about my morning's work and very casually asking her to show me a sign that she was safe and happy. While I am not a particularly religious person, I consider myself as being spiritually aware, and I inherently know that what happened next was orchestrated by Donna.

An incredibly beautiful, small, lilac, butterfly landed on my lower arm and remained there for several minutes. As I thanked whoever or whatever had delivered the butterfly as proof of Donna's existence, I was overcome with joyous emotion on a level that I had never experienced before. Tears of emotion followed, and every hair on my arms and on the back of my neck stood up with a steadfast certainty. Within minutes, I had contacted Donna's family with the news. What was not lost on any of us was the fact that this butterfly was lilac; lilac was Donna's favourite colour, and her love of the colour extended to literally anything: decor, clothes, shoes, and accessories, to mention only a few examples. I have often challenged myself as to whether my description of this petite butterfly as lilac is correct, as while blue butterflies are native to this country, I had never before or since seen a lilac butterfly. I have scoured books on British wildlife, but I have never found a moth or a butterfly that resembles what came and spent time on my arm that day. It remains a mystery, but for what it is worth my belief is that Donna was able to confirm her existence to me that day. I did not have any barriers to her demonstration unlike her family whose desperate need for proof somehow got in the way.

I have at various times been led to believe that sometimes when the emotions are so heightened following the death of a loved one, it is not unusual for a connection to be made with a person who is not so heavily affected by intense emotions. I feel blessed that on this and several other occasions I have been the one to share in these miracles. It has been a true honour that I have personally shared with these unique, beautiful souls their presence for a moment in time. It is proof in my eyes (and I acknowledge that many of you will disagree) that while our physical life does indeed cease our soul is able to transcend our physical reality and move on to another non-physical existence.

Afterword

Well hopefully you're still with me and haven't felt the need to skip to the end, because if that is the case then you have missed out on the life events of a group of true characters. Each one has touched my life in some shape or form, contributing in their unique way and exposing me to a full range of emotions. It hopefully has given you, the reader, a glimpse into the lives of a cross-section of a community, and, as such, serves as an example of how we all face our own trials and tribulations as human beings.

What I attempted to do was to choose a group of patients that offer us the opportunity to reflect on how dominant behaviours affect the lives of patients, their loved ones, and the staff involved in their care. Challenging behaviours are without doubt difficult to deal with at times for all of us. Modern living places so many demands on our time that we do not always reflect on that which is important to us.

I am yet to sit with a patient at the end of his or her life whose comments are that they wish they had spent more time at work, and yet that is where our loyalties appear to rest in many cases. Chronic overworking, whether paid or unpaid, has a lot to answer for. While we remain a society that invests so much importance in our working lives there is little space to focus on our own needs.

What patients do almost unanimously share with me as they reflect on their lifetime is that they wish they had been more loving, as a parent, a brother, a sister, a child, a partner, and to him or herself in many instances. It never ceases to amaze me how many tears are shed at the end of a life regarding the missed opportunities to demonstrate how much we love our family and friends. I have lost track of the number of people who have expressed a wish to either demonstrate their forgiveness of someone's past misdemeanour or who are desperate to be forgiven for a misdeed that they feel responsible for. In the cold light of day it is a staggering and sobering fact that so many of us place more significance on work than we do on demonstrating loving kindness.

One of the saddest sights that I have witnessed over the years is that of an unfulfilled life.'Don't die with your music still left in you' Dr Wayne Dyer, always springs to mind when I listen to the patients' regrets about their lifetimes. It has served as a great incentive in my life to prioritise that which is important and to identify what makes my 'heart sing'.

To spend time in the presence of one who expresses positive emotions of gratitude, joy, compassion, forgiveness, and love not only raises the mood and energy of him or herself and others, but also contributes to the positive healing environment that they co-create by their attitude. This is not to suggest that illness is not without major challenges that place people in very fearful and vulnerable situations that require courage, trust, and hope.

During the previous chapters I am sure you will agree that what stands out is the essential need to establish and maintain nurse-patient relationships that are built on belief and trust. A growing area of interest among scientists, the medical and nursing professions, and those seeking spiritual solutions to unhealthy behaviours is self-love in relation to achieving a balanced, healthy lifestyle. In many respects it should not come as a surprise that self-love is essential to our health? It is hardly rocket science to assume that to love one's self is actually the bedrock of being able to extend the same to others.

Unfortunately, it has largely been accepted that self-love is a form of self-indulgence and is a selfish act.

Our individual influences as a child will largely shape how and if we even acknowledge self-love. You may be familiar with the following phrase, 'Give me a child for his first seven years, and I'll give you the man.'—Jesuit maxim. Despite there still being debate over the actual author and the exact date of the quote, what is fact is that we are considering a quote between four and five hundred years old. Interestingly, Bruce Lipton, eminent, internationally renowned biologist, recently stated that a child from the years of one to six is in a hypnogogic state, which means that he or she absorbs everything we tell them. Even the negative, for example, 'You are stupid and unlovable,' said by a significant other becomes embedded in their unconscious. This will continue to affect the way he or she will think for the rest of his or her life. So despite the difference of four to five hundred years the facts remain the same. What we experience in our first seven years is largely going to affect the way we view the world, including how we feel about ourselves.

My own thoughts on these revealing facts are that this research-based information should be brought to the attention of those who take responsibility for planning the nurse training curriculum, and they should be included in all future training programmes. Trainees should be given the opportunity to conduct an inquiry into the significance of self-love. Not only would such an inquiry help nurses to ensure that they have considered their own relationship with self-love, but it would help us reflect upon the behaviours of those within our care.

With a greater understanding regarding the above there comes a deeper appreciation about why so many of us, including myself, persist in exposing ourselves regularly to unhealthy coping methods. I have certainly changed my approach to care towards myself and to others by studying this subject. I still of course react at times in a judgemental manner without being aware of all the history leading up to that point in time, but I am able to extend compassion and forgiveness more readily now, as I have learnt to do the same to myself.

We are often our own worse critics, and many of us treat ourselves diabolically. Our internal chatter directed at ourselves is often far harsher than we would subject ourselves to by another. We become accustomed over time to think that it is an acceptable way to treat ourselves.

Why?

The reasons lie in that negative internal chatter becomes habitual behaviour that we choose (believe it or not) to repeat time after time. Giving ourselves a really hard time is for many of us a regular pastime: 'God, you look fat in that'; 'your hair is horrible'; 'You're ugly.'

The majority of us wouldn't dream of repeating such things to a good friend, but we pass the comments to ourselves over and over again.

Madness, isn't it?

The good news is that with a bit of practice we can teach one another as human beings that we have a choice over our thoughts. Like any new behaviour, it takes time, commitment, and tenacity, but it leads to amazing results.

When I first heard and read about self-love, I thought that it was not for the likes of me and mine. I was so wrong, however, and I am glad that I was.

I still battle on a daily basis with a part of me that wants nothing more than for me to remain a sceptic, but the difference now is that there is a voice within me that knows the truth. Love is what I'm made of; it is the real me, regardless of whether I subscribe to this truth or not.

With growing scientific proof and highly respected authors choosing to write prolifically on the subject, I leave you with one wish I have for each and every one of you: 'Know that you are loved more than you can ever comprehend.'

Until the next time, reclaim your birth right; you deserve it.

About the author

Zoë C Lloyd is an experienced District Nursing sister, in addition to being the Chief Executive Officer of <u>www.beehappynow.co.uk,</u> a Stress Management training company specialising in work with general medical practice. She lives in Sandbach, Cheshire, England with her partner, Jan, and their four rescue dogs.